Wild Faith

DEVOTIONAL FOR KIDS

To Josh, for walking with me
on this wild journey of faith
and listening to so very
many animal facts. I love you.
—VE

For Mom and Dad.
—JB

WATERBROOK

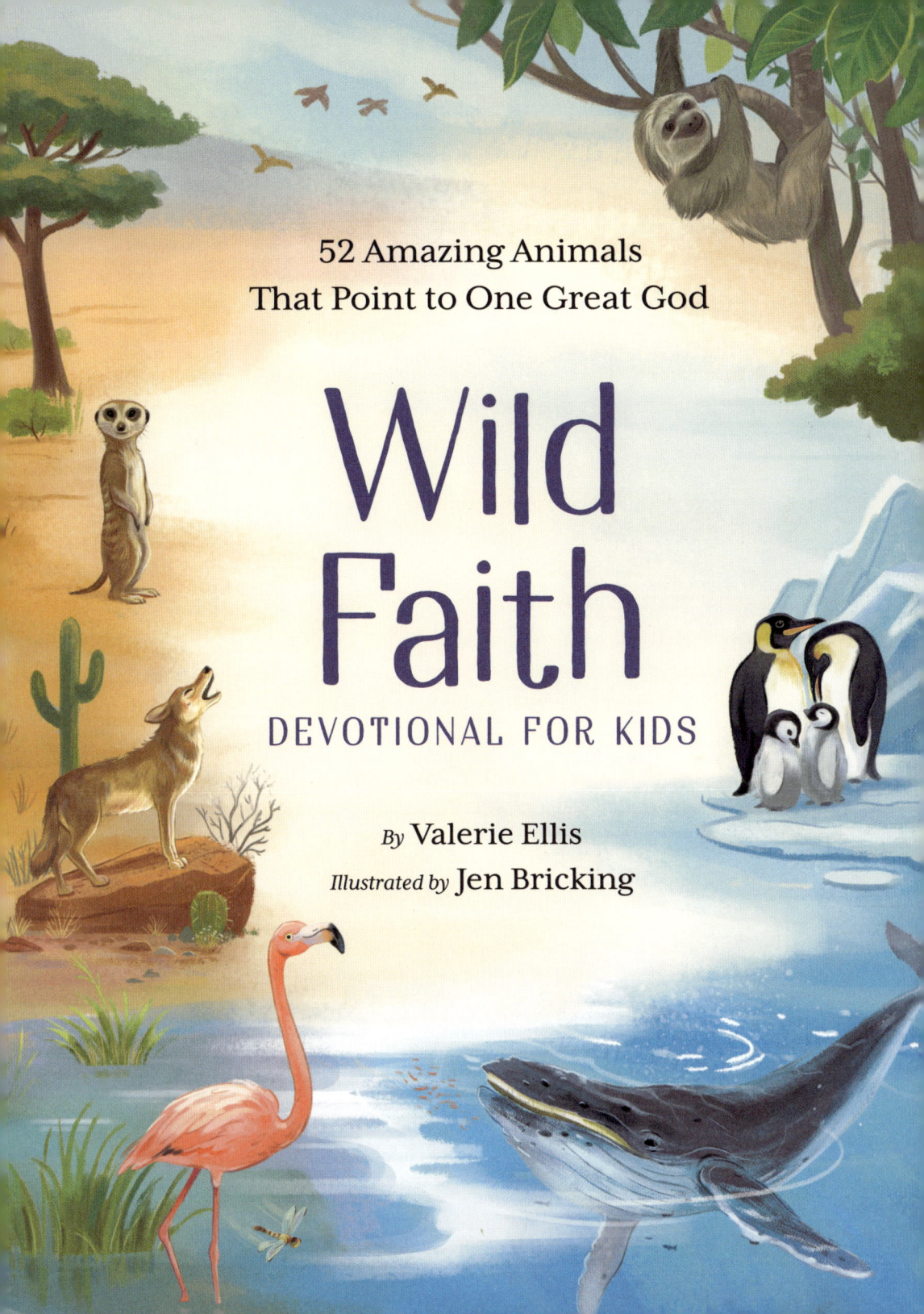

52 Amazing Animals
That Point to One Great God

Wild
Faith

DEVOTIONAL FOR KIDS

By Valerie Ellis

Illustrated by Jen Bricking

Contents

WELCOME TO
Wild Faith

The heavens proclaim the glory of God.
　　The skies display his craftsmanship.
Day after day they continue to speak;
　　night after night they make him known.
They speak without a sound or word;
　　their voice is never heard.
Yet their message has gone throughout the earth,
　　and their words to all the world.

—PSALM 19:1-4, NLT

God created the world. And though creation can never fully express the wonders of the Lord, sometimes examples from nature can make God's truth come alive to us.

This is why I've gathered fifty-two amazing animals for you to explore and learn from. I loved digging into the research, and I hope that with each animal, you'll not only marvel at how awesome God is but also discover more about the incredible life He invites you to! Saying "yes" to God isn't always comfortable and easy, but it's absolutely worth it.

In this devotional, each animal gives you a chance to understand God more and grow in your love for Him. You'll increase your knowledge of Scripture through key verses. You'll also be encouraged to "Make It Stick" and "Live It Out" through interactive reflections, questions, prayers, and more.

As you read, I want you to remember two important things. They may seem like opposites, but I promise they work *together* to help us grow:

1. As hard as we may try, we need God's help to live lives that please Him. He knows we can't be perfect, and He never meant for us to do it on our own. He wants us to rely on His grace and strength at every step.

2. God is always there to guide and help us, but He won't *make* us do anything. To live the fulfilling lives He has planned for us, we need to choose to seek His ways, follow His direction, and stay close to Him.

It's not one or the other. It's both! Choosing to follow Him and trusting that God's got you.

So whether you use this devotional daily, weekly, or whenever you need some inspiration, let's bravely follow our faithful God, who calls us to a good path and helps us every step of the way. As you encounter these fifty-two awesome animals, may you celebrate God's creativity, seek Him with all your heart, and rest in His great love for you.

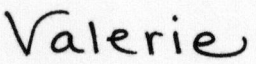

Valerie

Saying "Yes" to God's Best Gift

It's fascinating to see God's creativity in everything He made: daisies, dirt, stars, snakes, honeybees, humpback whales, and *you*!

But one way God set humans apart is by making us in His own image. We are created to reflect His character.

> God said, "Let us make human beings in our image, to be like us."
>
> **—GENESIS 1:26,** NLT

And one incredible part of being made in God's image is that God wants us to have a special relationship with Him.

You see, humans are designed to experience God's amazing love and follow His life-giving ways. But starting with the first two humans ever created, people decided to ignore His plan. They wanted to do things their own way instead of honoring and obeying Him. That choice is called sin, and when sin came into the world, it caused all kinds of sadness and brokenness. Creation no longer worked perfectly. People stopped living peacefully. And most importantly, sin harmed the special relationship between people and God.

To this day, we see the effects of sin in the world around us and in our own hearts. We all think and act in ways that don't please God.

> All have sinned and fall short of the glory of God.
>
> **—ROMANS 3:23**, CSB

But here's the good news: Sin doesn't change God's love! He still wants to be close to us.

He knows we need to be rescued from the broken ways of sin. But He also knows that no human could ever do enough good things to rescue themselves and earn His forgiveness. So He came up with a solution.

God sent His Son, Jesus, into the world to make everything right again.

> The wages of sin is death, but the gift of God is eternal life in Christ Jesus our Lord.
>
> **—ROMANS 6:23**, CSB

Jesus was born in Bethlehem. He grew up, lived a perfect life, and showed people what God is like. He taught, healed, and loved. He was full of grace and truth.

Then Jesus died on the cross.

But that wasn't the end. After three days, Jesus rose to life again! He died for our sins to bring us back to God. He rose again to give us new life and show that sin and death are defeated. His victory gives us hope that one day everything will be restored to God's perfect design. Nothing can stop God! Nothing can change His love for us!

> God loved the world in this way: He gave his one and only Son, so that everyone who believes in him will not perish but have eternal life.
> —JOHN 3:16, CSB

We are still waiting for the day when Jesus will return and everything will work perfectly again. But we *don't* have to wait to enjoy a special relationship with God.

Do you believe that God is the king of everything and that life works best when people love Him and follow His ways? Do you recognize that sometimes you don't choose to follow God's ways and that you need His forgiveness? Do you believe that Jesus died on the cross and rose again to provide the way back to a wonderful relationship with God? Do you want to trust Jesus and follow Him as the Lord of your life?

Then you can start this life-changing relationship now. Talk with God about your responses to the questions you just read. Thank Him for His love and for His free gift of forgiveness and rescue through Jesus. Tell God you want to follow Jesus and live for Him.

If you confess with your mouth, "Jesus is Lord," and believe in your heart that God raised him from the dead, you will be saved.

—ROMANS 10:9, CSB

Jesus promised that all who trust in Him have eternal life. And He is preparing a perfect home for us where we can live with Him forever. But eternal life starts now! With the help of God's Holy Spirit, we can find joy and purpose as we follow Jesus and try to live according to God's design. We won't be perfect, but we can always count on the Lord's grace and power to help us.

You are saved by grace through faith, and this is not from yourselves; it is God's gift—not from works, so that no one can boast. For we are his workmanship, created in Christ Jesus for good works, which God prepared ahead of time for us to do.

—EPHESIANS 2:8-10, CSB

If you made the decision to follow Jesus, tell a friend or adult who loves Jesus too. They can encourage you and help you on your journey. This is just the beginning.

Soak It Up!

FLAMINGO

May the God of hope fill you with all joy and peace as you trust in him, so that you may overflow with hope by the power of the Holy Spirit.

—ROMANS 15:13

Flamingos have a secret: They're not really pink (at least, not without some help). Flamingos are born with white and gray feathers. They get their pink color from what they eat—like algae and brine shrimp. Their bodies absorb the nutrients, depositing pink color in their feathers. What goes inside shows on the outside! In fact, scientists say the pinker a flamingo, the healthier it is.

You've probably heard a parent or teacher say to include healthy foods in what you eat so you can grow stronger. Taking in the right food can help us feel better and help our bodies work properly. In that sense, we're just like flamingos: We can be healthy on the outside only when we're well nourished on the inside. And this is important not just for our physical bodies but for our spiritual lives too.

When we feed on God's Word and spend time with Him, we absorb His truth and love. These get dropped into our hearts and minds and show on the outside as joy, patience, helpfulness, and perseverance. The more we take in what is healthy for our spirits, the more those good things will show up in our attitudes and actions.

For example, when we focus on gratitude inside instead

of anger, it's easier to show kindness to others. When we're filled with God's peace instead of anxiety, we're more likely to make wise choices. And when our hearts are flooded with truths such as "God is near," it's so much easier to get through life's challenges with hope and strength.

So just like a flamingo takes in what it needs to be healthy, let's soak up God's pure love and nourishing truth each day. We can fill up on God's best for us and let Him renew us from the inside out!

Make It Stick *Imagine God's love is your favorite color and, as you absorb it, you become that color from the inside out. What color would you be?*

Live It Out *Write down one way you can take in nourishment from God this week (and make sure you're specific by including a time and place too):*

_____

_____

Take notice of the ways His love is showing up in your attitudes and actions, and thank Him for nourishing and strengthening you.

Fun Fact
Flamingos can stand on one leg. They can sleep that way too!

Created and Cared For

GIRAFFE

I will praise you
because I have been remarkably and
  wondrously made.
Your works are wondrous,
and I know this very well.

—PSALM 139:14, CSB

Did you know that a group of giraffes can be called a herd, a tower, or a journey? And did you know that even though giraffes in a herd may look similar, each of them is unique? Their coats are as different as human fingerprints. God designs each beautiful giraffe to be completely original.

In fact, although many animals that live in groups

seem to blend together, when you look more closely, you realize just how special each one is.

God places every hair, from head to hoof, with intention. And He created *you* with even more love and care.

When Jesus wanted to explain how valuable we are, He said God even knows the number of hairs on our heads (LUKE 12:7). That is mind-blowing because it's impossible for any human to count their hairs. Plus, the number of hairs we have is always

changing! But God knows how many hairs we have, because He created each strand with remarkable care. And if He notices this tiny detail of who we are, we can trust that He watches over every part of us—our bodies, our minds, and our hearts.

Yep! God sees you as a special individual, not just a face in the crowd. He cares about the big things in your life and the small things. He understands your dreams and struggles. He knows what brings you joy and what makes you anxious. God even knows your favorite pizza topping (or if you like pizza at all)!

So next time you think of a journey of spotted giraffes, remember that God crafted you uniquely and cares for you completely. You are His wonderful, treasured creation!

Live It Out 〉 *Give yourself a hug. Thank God that He made you wonderfully and always watches over you.*

Make It Stick 〉 *Now go find someone else to encourage—with a hug, a high five, a note, a kind word, or any other way you can think of—because everyone needs a reminder of how wonderfully God made them!*

Famously
Friendly

CAPYBARA

Follow God's example, therefore, as dearly loved children
and walk in the way of love, just as Christ loved us.

—EPHESIANS 5:1–2

Capybaras are famously friendly animals! These giant South American rodents often let other animals, like squirrel monkeys or wattled jacana birds, sit or ride on their backs.

But what is it about capybaras that makes other creatures want to hang out with them? Maybe it's their warm fur. Or their calm presence. Or maybe it's how they work together to protect their herd. Whatever the reason, God wants us to be like the capybara and create an inviting environment that welcomes others to hang out with us too!

Jesus was known for being welcoming. He invited people to be with Him, even those who were ignored by others. He let people interrupt Him, and He met their needs. And crowds of people wanted to be with Him!

This world can be a hard place sometimes. Everyone wants to belong and to feel safe. As believers, we can be like Jesus and extend God's love to all people.

So how will others know we're safe, kind people to be with? Communicating warmth and welcome

Fun Fact
Capybaras are the largest rodents in the world—twice as big as beavers.

starts with the simple things: eye contact, a smile, and a friendly tone of voice. We can show even more friendliness as we encourage people, help them with problems, and treat them as Jesus would. We can also learn more about their interests and try to find things we have in common. The little things we do to show we care can make a big difference.

Let's remember the welcoming ways of Jesus. Inspired by God's kindness, we can offer friendship to those who need it most.

Make It Stick ⸾ *Pretend you're sitting next to Jesus on a comfy sofa and feeling the warmth of His love. Thank Him for being a welcoming place.*

Live It Out ⸾ *This week, think of one way you can be a friend to someone. And then do it!*

Free to Grow

S N A K E

Brothers and sisters, I do not consider myself to have taken hold of it. But one thing I do: Forgetting what is behind and reaching forward to what is ahead, I pursue as my goal the prize promised by God's heavenly call in Christ Jesus.

—PHILIPPIANS 3:13–14, CSB

A snake's skin can't grow.

Wait—what? Does that mean a snake is stuck being the same size forever?

No way! A snake can actually shed that too-tight skin, revealing a new layer of skin and leaving the old layer behind. This process is called ecdysis (**ek**-duh-suhs), and it also helps the snake get rid of parasites and worn-out scales. But it's a lot of work. A snake often needs help from nearby trees and rocks as it gets rid of its old skin. Yet even with all the struggles, the process is totally worth it. The snake is able to grow—just as God designed!

Sometimes *we* also need to shed old things so we can grow. We may need to leave behind certain habits or ways of thinking so we can become the people God wants us to be. When we put aside what no longer fits God's plan for us, we can grow more like Jesus and experience God's best.

Even when it's hard, growing is worth it for us too. Shedding the old and embracing the new feels great once we do it. And just like the snake gets help, we can count on God to provide what we need! Whatever it is you want to shed, you can look for God's help by getting tips from a parent or teacher, memorizing a Bible verse, asking a friend for prayer, and counting on God to give you grace and strength.

So when we notice an attitude or habit that is keeping us stuck, let's remember how good it is to grow. We can be confident that what God asks us to do, He helps us do! He is always there to guide us to new places of growth.

Fun Fact

A snake may go through ecdysis four to twelve times a year. Young snakes shed more often than adults since they are growing faster.

Make It Stick } Act out wriggling out of a too-tight skin. Thank God that He helps us grow!

Live It Out } Whenever you notice that an old habit or attitude is holding you back, try this: Thank the Holy Spirit for bringing it to your attention, and ask the Lord to help you change. Don't get discouraged if it takes time. Just keep going back to God, knowing He is patient.

Expert Tasters

CATFISH

Taste and see that the LORD is good.
How happy is the person who takes refuge in him!

—PSALM 34:8, CSB

What if you could taste with more than just your mouth? That's what catfish do! Catfish have taste buds *all over* their bodies—even on their backs, bellies, and barbels.

And catfish don't just have a lot of taste buds. They have really strong ones. These powerful taste buds are important because many catfish hunt in murky waters, where it's hard to see. Their taste buds help them find the food they need to thrive.

The Bible says, "Taste and see that the LORD is good," but it doesn't mean lick your Bible. (Ewww.) Tasting is a way to experience something—to take it in and learn about it. So "tasting" the Lord means we discover and appreciate how wonderful He is and take in His goodness.

Life gets murky sometimes, but we can teach our hearts and minds to taste the kindness of the Lord all around us. Like when we . . .

- Notice daily blessings: A smile, a kind word, and even the sweet smell of flowers are gifts from God to us.
- Pray: We can't see God, but He's closer than our best friend. And we can talk with Him and feel that nearness anytime through prayer.

barbel

- Look for helping hands: When things are tough, we can see God working through the people He sends to help us. And when we feel the desire to help someone, that's God working in us too!

How wonderful to have a strong sense of taste when it comes to noticing God's caring ways! Just like the catfish is an expert taster in murky waters, we can be *supertasters* of God's love and kindness, even when things are confusing or difficult.

And similar to when we eat our favorite foods, once we taste God's goodness, we won't want to stop.

Fun Fact
At least seven species of catfish swim upside down!

Make It Stick

Think of one example of God's goodness. If it had a flavor, what would it be?

Live It Out

Sometimes noticing God's care takes practice and teamwork. Challenge your family to taste God's goodness this week. Then share what you experienced each day.

Sing It Out!

C O Y O T E

Trust in him at all times, you people;
pour out your hearts to him,
for God is our refuge.

—PSALM 62:8

Coyotes are so common in the United States that people have all kinds of nicknames for them. One nickname is "song dog." That's because coyotes make so many different sounds to share information and attract attention. Some scientists believe that their wide array of yips, barks, huffs, howls, and even bark-howls express surprise, distress, longing, joy, security, anger, and more.

Humans also experience many emotions every day. Some feelings we welcome, like excitement and peace. Other emotions, like anger and sadness, we may try to push away. Sometimes we feel calm and content. And other times, completely overwhelmed.

Just like God gave song dogs many sounds to "sing" about how they feel or what they need, people in the Bible also sang to express their feelings! In fact, right in the middle of the Bible, God tucked in a beautiful gift: the book of Psalms. (*Psalms* is another word for "songs.")

The psalms written so long ago can help us today. People wrote songs to remember God's goodness and express joy and gratitude. They also wrote songs to bring their sadness, frustration, worry, and confusion to God. When we read the book of Psalms, we can discover words to express our own feelings and find reminders that God is always with us—no matter what emotions we feel.

Psalms are the Bible-time version of the worship songs we hear at church. Both help us praise God, ask for strength, and seek His comfort. Whether modern or ancient, songs can lead us to our caring God.

So whatever you're feeling—happy, sad, surprised, or upset—try taking inspiration from the book of Psalms and sing a song! And if singing isn't your thing, you can write in a journal, share your feelings with a trusted adult or friend, or pray about your feelings. With God's help, you can find healthy ways to figure out and deal with your emotions.

Make It Stick 〗 *Grab a sheet of paper (or use the blank space below) and draw a heart. Then draw a circle around the heart. Use this image as a reminder that God cares about all your emotions.*

Live It Out 〗 *Do you have a favorite worship song from church or that your family listens to at home or in the car? Try singing it (in your head or out loud) the next time you're facing big feelings. Don't have a favorite yet? This week, pay attention to which songs encourage your heart.*

Steady Steps

KLIPSPRINGER

The LORD makes firm the steps
of the one who delights in him.

—PSALM 37:23

When your name means "rock leaper," jumping is a given. But a klipspringer is more than your average hopper.

This small African antelope has strong hind legs that help it jump ten feet straight up in the air. Not only that, but all four of its hooves can also land on a space no bigger than a saltine cracker! These incredible skills come in handy on the rocky hills where the klipspringer lives. It's steady on the roughest ground. That's how it can stay safe from less nimble predators and forage for food in the trickiest places.

Sometimes in life, our path is also rocky and rough. We face hard choices and go through tough situations. But no matter what, we can trust God and the guidance we find in His Word. After all, He made us and He made the world, so He knows how life works best. In His kindness, God gave us the Bible—our instruction book for how to live. And when we depend on it,

Fun Fact

Big jumps are often hard on an animal's bones and joints. To absorb the impact of its leaps, God gave klipspringers cylinder-shaped hooves that are firm on the outside and rubbery on the inside.

Scripture promises that we will have peace and be steady through even the hardest circumstances. We can stay sure-footed like the klipspringer!

But it's not enough to just *hear* God's instructions. We've got to *love* His instructions and *obey* them. That's what keeps us peaceful and secure. Sometimes we might feel tempted to follow an easier or more popular way, but when we trust what the Bible says, we know we are in a stable place. Because what God says never fails!

Let's strengthen ourselves with God's Word each day. Though life may be as rough and scary as a rocky cliffside, God's instructions can keep us as steady as a klipspringer.

Make It Stick *Stand on one foot for as long as you can, and time yourself. How long did you make it? Now stand on one foot while holding on to a wall or table. Much easier, right? That's how it is when we rely on God's Word to steady us!*

Live It Out *Here's a great way to love and treasure God's Word—know it by heart. Write down our key verse (PSALM 37:23) and tape it somewhere you'll notice it often (like on the bathroom mirror). After you've memorized that verse, try another one, such as PSALM 119:165.*

Teamwork Makes the Dream Work

MEERKAT

Use whatever gift you've received for the good of one another so that you can show yourselves to be good stewards of God's grace in all its varieties.

—1 PETER 4:10, VOICE

Meerkats are excellent at teamwork. They take turns doing different jobs to help the group thrive in the desert. Some get food. (They love to eat beetles, spiders, and scorpions.) Some watch the baby meerkats and keep them safe. (These meerkats may not eat until it's their time to hunt). And one or more act as lookouts and warn the others of danger. Meerkats also team up to dig bolt-holes, where they can hide from predators.

By working together, the meerkat group grows stronger. Everyone joins in, and every job is needed.

In the family of God, each person can do something to strengthen the group. Using the gifts and talents we've received from the Lord, we can serve food, sing songs, teach the Bible, clean up, write encouraging notes, or pray with friends in need. Just like the meerkats switch jobs, we don't always have to do the same thing. But no matter how we help, we can be sure that every job matters as we work together to serve the Lord.

Maybe you've never thought of yourself as part of something bigger, but you are. You're part of the family of God. You're a member of the body of Christ,

the community God made where everyone can contribute and grow.

The meerkat group reminds us that God wants us to work as a team. It's exciting when teams pull together for a common goal! And we can team up to care for one another and show the world what God is like.

Whatever gifts God has given you, know that you can use them to honor Him and bless the people around you. As we work together, just imagine what we can accomplish for His kingdom.

Make It Stick *Shout out, "Go, team!" And thank God that He made us to work together.*

Live It Out *Talk with your parents or church leaders about how you can start serving in your church or community right now.*

Fun Fact
Many young animals learn from watching the adults, but meerkats take it a step further. Grown-up meerkats actively teach young meerkats to handle tricky prey, even scorpions.

Surprising Source of Strength

ANT

I will boast all the more gladly about my weaknesses, so that Christ's power may rest on me. That is why, for Christ's sake, I delight in weaknesses, in insults, in hardships, in persecutions, in difficulties. For when I am weak, then I am strong.

—2 CORINTHIANS 12:9-10

Many people assume that because ants are small, they are weak. But did you know that some ants can lift fifty times their body weight? If humans could do that, we'd be lifting cars, no problem.

It might seem bizarre that a creature so tiny could be so strong, but an ant's power is possible *because* of its small size.

That's because as a creature gets bigger, the weight of its muscles increases faster than its strength. And when a creature lifts something, it's not just lifting the object—it's lifting all that muscle too.

So basically, it's almost always easier for little animals, and not large animals, to lift objects that are much heavier than they are. Surprise!

We can be tempted to think that facing problems on our own makes us strong. But we are actually *weaker* when we put on a tough face and act like we can handle everything solo. How do we get stronger? By remembering we need God's help. When we acknowledge our weakness and rely on God, we gain power. It's amazingly opposite!

That's what the apostle Paul was talking about in today's key verses (2 CORINTHIANS 12:9–10). He knew that God was the source of his strength. In fact, he was grateful for the struggles that reminded him to rely on God.

Both the tiny ant and Paul's example give us hope and reveal the astonishing truth about strength in God's kingdom. We don't have to try to look or act big and tough. Because when we trust God in our weakness, He makes us strong—stronger than we ever thought we could be!

Make It Stick 〉〉 Flex your arm muscles and thank God that He gives us an even better kind of strength in our hearts when we call on Him.

Live It Out 〉〉 Think about a situation you're going through right now where you need God to give you strength. What is hard about it? Tell the Lord. In your weakness, He can make you strong.

Fun Fact
There are more than twelve thousand types of ants, and ants live on every continent except Antarctica.

Heavy-Duty Coat of Patience

SEA OTTER

My dear brothers and sisters, take note of this:
Everyone should be quick to listen, slow to speak and
slow to become angry, because human anger does
not produce the righteousness that God desires.

—JAMES 1:19-20

Imagine you and seven of your friends take all the hair you have on your heads and pack it into a single inch. That's how dense a sea otter's coat is! Sea otters have two layers of the thickest fur of any animal on earth. When kept clean, these two layers trap air bubbles for a protective layer of warmth in the chilly ocean. In fact, as the sea otter grooms its thick fur, it even blows air into its coat.

Sea-otter fur has other waterproof features too. The sea otter spreads natural oils from its skin through the fur as it grooms, and the shape of each tiny hair helps the hairs interlock to form a barrier. Some furry animals get soaked to the skin as soon as they jump into the water. But when water touches the sea otter's fur, it just rolls off.

God has given His children a gift that works like the sea otter's remarkable coat: patience!

Unfortunately, people are going to do and say things that are rude and insensitive. They will have different opinions and may even get the facts wrong. But we don't have to react in anger or take their unkind words to heart. We can wrap

Fun Fact

Sea otters can sleep while floating. To stay together, they sometimes wrap themselves in kelp or hold hands in their sleep.

ourselves in the warmth of God's patience—like a sea otter's cozy, waterproof coat—and let the little frustrating things just roll off us.

It's wise to let some things go, but other problems are worth working through. In those times, the Bible says to be quick to listen, slow to speak, and slow to get angry (JAMES 1:19). This can be hard, but showing patience demonstrates respect for the other person. And it's good for our hearts too. The Bible even says that when we're patient, people will take note of our wisdom and it will bring us honor (PROVERBS 19:11).

Patience takes practice, but the goodness it brings into our lives is worth it!

IMPORTANT NOTE: If someone is bullying or harming you or someone else, that is not to be ignored. Share with a trusted adult, and talk about ways you can get the help you need.

Make It Stick 〉〉 Clench your fists like you're angry, and then slowly release them. As you feel the muscles in your hands relax, whisper, "God, please help me be quick to listen, slow to speak, and slow to become angry."

Live It Out 〉〉 Even if you don't find yourself in a tough situation this week, you can still practice patience. When talking with family or friends, try to learn something about their point of view before jumping in with your own idea or opinion. It's great practice for when those tougher times come.

Good Move!

BLUE WILDEBEEST

migration from Tanzania to Kenya

The LORD is the one who will go before you. He will be with you; he will not leave you or abandon you. Do not be afraid or discouraged.

—DEUTERONOMY 31:8, CSB

The blue wildebeest's migration is celebrated as one of the most awe-inspiring events in the natural world.

As the dry season starts in East Africa, the wildebeest's ideal food begins to run low. So they make the long journey north. They travel about five hundred miles across plains and through crocodile-infested rivers to find more plentiful food. After several months, when the rains start to replenish their original grazing grounds, they return for their favorite meals.

Just like the wet and dry seasons cause wildebeest to migrate, seasons in our lives spark changes too. And not just holiday seasons or weather seasons. We also have life seasons. We may have a season of hanging out with a certain group of friends, going to a particular school, or doing a favorite activity. But then things change.

Sometimes the change is outside our control—a friend moves or we graduate to a new school—but sometimes God guides us to *choose* something different. Perhaps our current spot has become unhealthy because our friends are making poor choices. Or maybe God has a new opportunity for us, such as a new skill He wants us to learn.

The wildebeest must migrate to survive, and we, too, may need a change to grow into the people God wants us to be. It may be hard to step out and leave what is familiar and comfortable, especially because we don't know what lies ahead. But if God is leading, we can be sure it's for our good.

No matter what season of life you're traveling through, trust God to lead you. Ask for His help when things become difficult. And remember, He's with you every step of the way.

Make It Stick } *Write down four changes or challenges you've been through so far in life. Then circle them and write "God is with me" over the whole thing.*

_____

_____

_____

_____

Live It Out } *Let's ask for God's guidance: "Strong and loving God, is there anything You want me to change in my life right now? Are there any new paths You want me to take? Help me sense Your direction and go when it's time."*

Fun Fact
Another name for the wildebeest is *gnu.* The *g* is silent, so it's pronounced like "new."

Fully Seen and Fully Loved

GLASS FROG

LORD, you have searched me and known me.
You know when I sit down and when I stand up;
you understand my thoughts from far away. . . .
This wondrous knowledge is beyond me.
It is lofty; I am unable to reach it.

—PSALM 139:1-2, 6, CSB

God gave glass frogs a fascinating feature: The skin on their bellies is see-through! It's so clear that the little frog's intestines, its bones, and even its beating heart are revealed and easy to observe.

Our hearts are also on display and easy for God to see. But when the Bible says He looks at our hearts (1 SAMUEL 16:7), it's not talking about the body part that beats in our chests. In God's Word, *heart* often refers to our thoughts, desires, character, or intentions.

Some people think they can keep their thoughts and plans from God. They know that their desires don't reflect His ways. But God doesn't want us to hide our hearts from Him. First of all, that would be a waste of energy since it's impossible to do. Second, hiding our hearts hurts our relationship with Him.

God knows we will some- times stray from His com- mands, but He never stops loving us. In fact, He looks at our hearts be- cause He wants to help us.

It can be hard to admit that our hearts aren't lining up with what God wants, but by not dealing with this mismatch, we end up even more hurt and sad. When we try to hide our failures, confusion, and tough emo- tions, they only tend to grow.

However, when we bring our whole selves to God, we can experience a sense of relief and allow Him to help us. What- ever we've done, whatever has been done to us, all the ways we try so hard—we can give it all to Him. We can have peace, knowing our struggles are in the hands of the One who will never leave us.

We should always feel free to bring everything in our hearts to our faithful God. Because just like we can see through the amazing glass frog's skin, God sees *us*—and He loves us no matter what.

Make It Stick ⦚ *Put both hands on your heart and remember that God knows you fully and loves you perfectly. Be still for a moment and rest in that marvelous truth.*

Live It Out ⦚ *Grab a blank sheet of paper and write down everything your heart is feeling, both good and bad. Fold the paper up and offer your words to God as a prayer. Thank God that whenever our hearts need His touch, He is there.*

A Nest of Love

BARN SWALLOW

Let's not allow ourselves to get fatigued doing good. At the right time we will harvest a good crop if we don't give up, or quit. Right now, therefore, every time we get the chance, let us work for the benefit of all, starting with the people closest to us in the community of faith.

—GALATIANS 6:9-10, MSG

Barn swallows can be found in more places throughout the world than any other species of swallow. In fact, they are one of the most common of *all* land birds.

But barn swallows have an *un*common behavior. Some of them stick around to help out! Usually once birds learn to fly, they are off to live on their own. But instead of moving on, some teen and adult barn swallows stay to strengthen the family by taking on some of the work. Those older siblings help their parents feed the newly hatched baby birds.

God wants us to help *our* families too, and there are many ways to do it. It can be as simple as clearing someone else's dinner plate from the table or helping find a lost toy. Or it may require more attention, like encouraging your brother or sister when they're sad, asking your parents what chores they need your help with, or surprising a family member with a card or drawing.

Since we're with our families a lot, it's common to forget to be grateful for one another. It's natural to think only of ourselves instead of looking for ways to help. But the beautiful thing about God is that His instructions are *better* than what is natural and *beyond* what is common.

He knows that part of what it takes to live a full, happy, healthy life is helping others. And, of course, this starts with the people in our homes!

Let's take care of one another and look for ways to bless our families, just like the barn swallows do. A little kindness goes a long way.

Make It Stick Think of someone in your home that you're especially grateful for. Give God thanks for blessing you with that person.

Live It Out Find a way to help this week without being asked. If you can, do your act of kindness right now! As you help, thank God that His kingdom is full of love and that He wants you to participate in it.

Fun Fact

Barn swallows are aerial insectivores. That means they catch most of the bugs they eat while flying.

Sense What Can't Be Seen

SHARK

I pray that the eyes of your heart may be enlightened in order that you may know the hope to which he has called you, the riches of his glorious inheritance in his holy people, and his incomparably great power for us who believe.

—EPHESIANS 1:18–19

You've heard of the five senses: sight, hearing, touch, smell, and taste. Sharks use the same five senses we do. But sharks can also sense electric fields!

Using the sense of electroreception, sharks can detect the electric fields that other animals produce when their hearts beat or their muscles move. That's one way sharks can figure out where those animals are, even the ones they can't see.

How amazing that sharks have access to a whole world of information that most other animals are completely unaware of!

We humans also have ways to understand the world beyond what we can see. Even though we don't see God with our physical eyes, we can understand things about Him and the spiritual world with the eyes of our hearts.

Using the eyes of our hearts, we can sense that God is with us, even when we feel alone. We remember that blessings don't come by accident but rather are good gifts from above. We believe there's hope, though we may not

be sure of our next steps. We know that God has the victory, even if it may look like evil is winning. And when we're seeing with the eyes of our hearts, we remember we're God's precious treasure.

We don't want to go through this life unaware of who God is or miss His presence all around us. And God doesn't want that either. That's one reason He gives us the Holy Spirit! God's Spirit helps us

know God better, gives us wisdom and power, and shows us how God is working in our world. When we pay attention to the Spirit, it's better than having another sense!

So let's ask the Holy Spirit to open the eyes of our hearts so we can not only sense but also fully experience the rich blessings available to us as followers of Jesus. Because God is more real than anything we can see with our eyeballs!

Make It Stick *Close your eyes and pick out something specific that you can hear, smell, taste, or feel. Did something jump out at you that you didn't notice before? When we use the eyes of our hearts, we'll notice more things too!*

Live It Out *Maybe you need to understand God better, see hope in hard times, or just notice more of His blessings. Focus on one area and ask the Holy Spirit to help you become more aware of God and celebrate His nearness. Thank God that He wants you to understand Him, even though you can't see Him.*

In the Shepherd's Care

SHEEP

The LORD is my shepherd, I lack nothing.
   He makes me lie down in green pastures,
he leads me beside quiet waters,
   he refreshes my soul.
He guides me along the right paths
   for his name's sake.

—PSALM 23:1–3

You may have heard that sheep aren't smart. But that's not true! Sheep can remember faces, mazes, and food sources. They show emotion and can pick up on the feelings of other sheep in the flock. They also learn quickly—sometimes in just two tries! Sounds like a pretty intelligent animal.

So why do such smart animals need a farmer or shepherd to care for them? Because even though sheep are smart, they are *not* self-sufficient. They can't survive on their own.

Sheep need a shepherd to keep them away from cliffs, protect them from predators, and lead them to fresh grass. Shepherds even guard sheep from stress because a stressed sheep may eat less and become ill.

Just like sheep need a shepherd, we need God. This comparison goes all the way back to the Bible. Jesus is called our Shepherd because He cares for us, protects us, and guides us to what is best for us. He even goes looking for us if we have turned the wrong way.

Fun Fact
Sheep often use the position of their ears to express their emotions.

But humans are known for trying to prove we can do things on our own. Throughout history, we've wanted to do things *our* way.

This "I can do it myself" attitude is so common that even when we decide to follow God's ways, we sometimes get the mistaken idea that God expects us to do it all on our own.

But that's not His plan! He is right here, ready to help us at every step.

Let's follow our faithful Shepherd and trust His loving care. He leads us on the right paths. He never leaves us. And when we follow Him, we will experience lives filled with the things that really matter.

Now, that's pretty smart!

Make It Stick ⟩ *Trace the path below with your finger and say, "My Good Shepherd leads me well." Hold on to this truth anytime life is feeling a bit twisty and loopy.*

Live It Out ⟩ *We can gain strength for following Jesus by remembering how He has already helped us. List three ways the Good Shepherd has cared for you, and return to your list whenever you need a reminder.*

1. _____

2. _____

3. _____

Shining Inside and Out

COMB JELLY

cilia

You are the light of the world. . . . Let your light shine before others, that they may see your good deeds and glorify your Father in heaven.

—MATTHEW 5:14, 16

Sunlight can't reach to the ocean's depths, but the dark underwater world still has amazing light sources: bioluminescent animals!

A wide variety of ocean creatures—including sea worms, jellyfish, shrimp, squid, and fish—make their own light when chemicals inside them come together and release energy. This light, called bioluminescence, helps animals do all kinds of things, like communicate, escape predators, and find food.

The comb jelly is one of these creatures that uses bioluminescence. But because comb jellies are found not only in the deep sea but also in the ocean's surface waters, these jellies actually give *two* types of light shows. If comb jellies are close to the surface, light hits rows of cilia (hairlike structures) and creates a shimmering rainbow effect. In the depths, where there is no light, their bioluminescence often glows bright blue or green—a light shining in the darkness.

We also have a light that helps us shine in the darkness—Jesus! Many people don't understand how good God is or how much He loves them. Their vision is clouded by all the confusion, sadness, and evil in this world. So when Jesus came to show what God is like, He called Himself the

light of the world (JOHN 8:12). And He called *us,* His followers, the light of the world too! We can help people see God
more clearly.

Our light comes from God, but we still have a very important part to play in this light reaching others. We must
choose to let it shine! We let our light shine by doing good
deeds for the world to see. When we're helpful, patient,
and generous, it's like bioluminescence bursting through
the darkness. We also reflect light—like the comb jelly's
dazzling rainbow—when we tell others what Jesus has
done for us.

How wonderful to be a light that leads people to God!

Let this truth sink in as you fill in the four blanks to complete our key verses:

You are the _____ of the world. . . .

Let your light _____ before others,

that they may see your _____

deeds and glorify your _____

in heaven. (MATTHEW 5:14, 16)

This week, how can you do good and glorify God? Maybe you could shine your light by donating toys or food for people who need them, helping clean up trash at a park or in a neighbor's yard, or giving a compliment to someone who is usually overlooked. Think of a few more ideas, and stay on the lookout for other ways to show God's love too.

Fun Fact

They might have similar names, but the comb jelly is *not* a type of jellyfish. Though both are made of watery gel, comb jellies are shaped differently and don't have stinging tentacles like jellyfish do (instead they have sticky tentacles or none at all). The two creatures also "poop" differently—jellyfish get rid of waste through their mouths while comb jellies excrete from their back ends, like humans!

Huddling Heroes

EMPEROR PENGUIN

Let us think of ways to motivate one another to acts of love and good works. And let us not neglect our meeting together, as some people do, but encourage one another, especially now that the day of his return is drawing near.

—HEBREWS 10:24-25, NLT

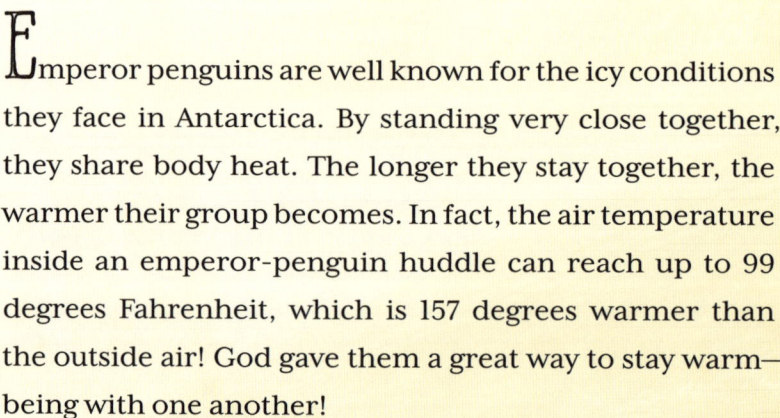

Emperor penguins are well known for the icy conditions they face in Antarctica. By standing very close together, they share body heat. The longer they stay together, the warmer their group becomes. In fact, the air temperature inside an emperor-penguin huddle can reach up to 99 degrees Fahrenheit, which is 157 degrees warmer than the outside air! God gave them a great way to stay warm—being with one another!

No matter what climate we live in, God wants us believers in Jesus to practice the same principle: Stand together and care for one another.

The world we face doesn't operate like God's very good kingdom. It can be harsh, cold, and unkind. But when Christians gather to encourage, teach, and help one another, it can be like the warmth of a cozy blanket or the protection of a penguin huddle.

Emperor penguins do another fascinating thing when they huddle: They shift around and take turns. Sometimes they're closer to the center— the warmest place—and sometimes they're closer to the edge— the coldest place.

There will be times when we struggle. Like penguins in the center of the huddle, we can surround ourselves with supportive people. Other times, God may be equipping us with the strength to stand in a colder place so we can provide more help and warmth to those who need it.

That's the beauty of God's design. He enables us to care and be cared for.

Make It Stick *Clasp your hands so all your fingers are warming one another up. Since you're now also in a great prayer pose, thank God for the support of others.*

Live It Out *How can you provide warmth to others this week? Or do you need support right now? Look for ways to give and receive encouragement.*

Fun Fact

Emperor penguins have sharp claws to grip the slippery ice. But sometimes they use their bellies to slide on it, like sleds on snow.

Gliding in Trust

C O L U G O

Don't worry about anything; instead, pray about everything.
Tell God what you need, and thank him for all he has done.
Then you will experience God's peace, which exceeds
anything we can understand. His peace will guard your
hearts and minds as you live in Christ Jesus.

—PHILIPPIANS 4:6–7, NLT

Y ou've probably heard of flying squirrels, but have you heard of this flying mammal? Like the flying squirrel, the colugo doesn't truly fly. It spreads its body to catch more air so that it glides to its destination. In fact, the colugo can soar two hundred feet because of a flap of skin that stretches from its chin out to its hands, feet, and tail.

Scientists aren't clear on all the reasons God gave the colugo this amazing ability, but one thing is for sure: Gliding through the air is a much quicker way to navigate treetops than climbing or crawling. Gliding also allows them to reach food that other animals can't and (this part isn't in the science books) is way more fun.

Just like hopping through the branches would slow down the colugo, worry can slow us down. The Bible tells us that worrying is a waste of time and energy. In fact, Jesus once asked His disciples a question that might seem silly but actually holds a lot of truth: "Can any one of you by worrying add a single hour to your life?" (MATTHEW 6:27). Of course not!

You can't exactly glide past problems and obstacles in life, but here's what you can do instead of worrying:

- Remember how much God loves you. If He feeds the birds and makes the flowers beautiful, you can be sure that He'll take care of you (MATTHEW 6:26–30).

- Seek God's kingdom first. Many things won't last, but living for God will always make a difference (VERSE 33).

- Give your worries to God. You can bring your concerns to Him and trust Him to handle them (1 PETER 5:7).

- Live fully every day. Worrying distracts. Trusting God makes room for the peace and joy He gives (JEREMIAH 17:7–8).

When you face a concern, think of the colugo gliding through the air. Ask God to help you move through this world without worrying.

Make It Stick 〟 *First, imagine the "worry" way: You're a colugo climbing through the trees. It's tricky and slow, and after all that, you can't even reach the food patch you want. Next, imagine the "trust God" way: You're a colugo smoothly gliding through the air to your yummy food.*

Live It Out 〟 *When worry comes to visit you, just tell it, "No, thanks. I know my God cares for me." And then give your worry to Him. Be patient with yourself and thank God that He has good plans for you.*

Fun Fact
The colugo is so skilled at gliding that it can even carry its baby while soaring through the air.

Seeking the Sun (Son)!

CABBAGE WHITE BUTTERFLY

Seek the LORD and his strength;
seek his presence continually!

—1 CHRONICLES 16:11, ESV

Y ou might be hot and sweaty or cold and shivering, but unless you're sick, your body keeps all your insides at just the right temperature. That's right—if you used a thermometer to take your *internal* body temperature, you would probably find it's right around where it always is: 98.6 degrees Fahrenheit.

However, for ectothermic (ek-tuh-**thur**-mik), or cold-blooded, animals, that's not the case. The body temperature of turtles, frogs, lizards, snakes, and fish changes based on how hot or cold their environment is. These animals need outside help to keep their insides healthy.

The cabbage white butterfly is one such creature. Many butterflies bask, or sunbathe, to absorb the sun's rays and warm their muscles enough to fly. But cabbage white butterflies use a unique kind of basking—reflectance basking—to make the most of the sun's heat. By opening their white wings partway and positioning themselves just

right, they can direct even more sunlight onto their bodies and more quickly get the energy they need. This is especially helpful on cloudy days!

People will sometimes say, "You have everything you need right inside you," or "Look inside yourself to find true happiness." But the truth is, just like butterflies, we *don't* have everything we need inside us. True peace, lasting strength, and fulfilling happiness come from Jesus. Looking for those things apart from Him will leave us frustrated, confused, or spending our lives on things that won't last.

Like cabbage white butterflies seek out sun to do what they can't do for themselves, we need to seek out Jesus, God's Son. And like they point their wings to warm up well, we can point our lives toward the Lord and experience all the good He has planned. After all, God is the source of life, the One who can give us just what we need.

Make It Stick *Stretch out your arms—like butterfly wings in the sun—and say our key verse (1 CHRONICLES 16:11) with joy.*

Live It Out *Let's pray to the Source of life: "Lord, thank You that You give the love, joy, and peace I could never muster up on my own. Help me seek You every day."*

Fun Fact
Butterfly wings can appear smooth, fuzzy, or even shimmery. But under a microscope, we can see they are made of tiny overlapping scales, like itty-bitty roof tiles!

No Room for Weeds

DUSKY FARMERFISH

The people who hear the word and receive it and grow in it—those are like the seeds sown on good soil. They produce a bumper crop, 30 or 60 or 100 times what was sown.

—MATTHEW 13:23, VOICE

Most people think only humans can garden and farm. But a few animals, like the dusky farmerfish, keep gardens too!

Dusky farmerfish live in the sea among coral reefs. They find patches of their favorite algae and take care of them. If other types of algae start to grow in their gardens, these farming fish treat them like weeds and toss them out. Why? The kind of algae these fish need won't grow as well if others crowd it.

God's truth is like seed for a garden. When we let it grow in our hearts, it produces all kinds of wonderful things, like strong faith that guides us through hard times, kindness that makes a difference, comforting peace, energizing joy, and calm patience.

But sometimes weeds try to come in and crowd out God's truth. In MATTHEW 13:22, Jesus said weeds are the worries of this life (the things that upset us so much we forget to trust God) and the lie of wealth (the belief that having more stuff is better and that pleasing ourselves is the most important thing).

It can be hard to keep weeds out of our gardens, because these types of messages are everywhere in our world. But we don't have to be discouraged. When we notice worry, distraction, and selfishness in our hearts, we can go to God—the master gardener. He will help us pull those weeds and grow a garden full of things that really matter.

Like the dusky farmerfish tosses out weeds, let's get rid of anything that crowds out God's truth. Let's grow a garden of faith and love in our hearts.

Make It Stick 〉 What's your favorite food that comes from a farm or garden? Thank God that farmers and gardeners keep the weeds away so delicious food can grow.

Live It Out 〉 What weeds might you need to pull to make sure your spiritual garden is healthy? Could you give a little less focus to things that won't last (worries, screens, other distractions) and a little more to things that will (healthy relationships, worship, helping your community)? If you're not quite sure what to do, pause and ask God to show you what's best.

Fun Fact

Like many fish in coral reefs, dusky farmerfish babies look very different from the adults. The young fish can be from yellow to brownish orange, and they have a dark area on their upper head and back. The adults are duller in color with a dark spot near their tail fin.

Helpers in the Waves

BOTTLENOSE DOLPHIN

In everything I did, I showed you that by this kind of hard work we must help the weak, remembering the words the Lord Jesus himself said: "It is more blessed to give than to receive."

—ACTS 20:35

Dolphins are focused on community. They cooperate with others in their group to make sure their pod survives and thrives. But dolphins don't look out only for their pod. They are famous for rescuing humans too. They even help animals that could never repay them, such as dogs and whales.

It's inspiring to know that God made dolphins to look out for anyone who needs help and to help unselfishly. We can be like that too.

The world is a big place. It can be tough out there in the waves of life! Sadly, sometimes people help only when they think they'll be repaid. But we show God's love in a special way when we help without expecting something in return. As our key verse reminds us, Jesus taught that it's better to give than to receive. He even said to search for those who *can't* repay you. Serve them, include them, and be kind to them, and God will repay you in heaven (LUKE 14:12–14).

Jesus lived it out too. He was always helping people no matter what! Even if the rest of the community looked

down on them or said they weren't important enough for Jesus to pay attention to, He still reached out to them. Throughout the countryside and in towns and cities, He cared for people's physical needs and tended to their hurting hearts.

Let's think of the dolphin and remember to do what Jesus did. We can help people no matter what and without looking for anything in return. And we won't have to wait until heaven for God to bless us. When we serve, we'll receive the joy of obeying our loving God, the benefit of growing closer to Jesus, and the privilege of making the world more like God's kingdom.

Make It Stick *Imagine you're swimming through the waves like a dolphin on a rescue mission. Ask God to help you grow more kind as you look for people to serve.*

Live It Out *Within the waves below, write down ways you could put Jesus's words into practice and serve someone in your community this week.*

Now go take action!

Armor Up!

PANGOLIN

Be strong in the Lord and in his mighty power.
Put on the full armor of God, so that you can
take your stand against the devil's schemes.

—EPHESIANS 6:10-11

The pangolin is the only mammal with scales. And those scales are an incredible form of protection. If the pangolin is ever in danger, it can roll up into an armored ball, safe and sound. Its scales are so tough that even top predators, like lions, usually give up and find something else to eat.

We have special armor too! Except ours protects us from the devil, life's ultimate predator, and helps us fight against his schemes. Ephesians 6:13–18 describes the six-piece suit of armor God has designed to protect our minds and our hearts in different ways.

We can stand firm when we keep God's truth close to

us like a belt and when we fasten His righteousness in place over our hearts like armor. The helmet of salvation guards our minds, while our faith in God becomes a shield that defends us from whatever the devil hurls at us. The good news about Jesus makes our feet ready for action, just as if we had on a great pair of shoes! And to fight back against evil? We have the sword of the Spirit, which is the Bible, God's Word. Prayer is also part of our battle plan, allowing us to stay in touch with our strong leader—Jesus.

And we shouldn't wait until we are tempted or have a crisis to put on the armor of God. We should gear up even on ordinary days so that when the devil strikes, we are ready to rely on God and rise above. Armor can work only if we put it on!

God gives the pangolin scales to help them stay safe from lions, and He provides a way for us to stand strong against the devil's destructive plans and fight back with what's good.

Make It Stick *Pretend to put on each piece of the armor of God. Then strike your best brave stance!*

Live It Out *Reread the third paragraph in the devotion. Underline one piece of God's armor you usually remember to put on. Circle one you want to get better at using this week.*

Fun Fact

In just one year, a pangolin might eat seventy million insects—and some of those critters bite! But the pangolin has special muscles to seal its nostrils and ears shut so its dinner doesn't hurt it.

Speedy Turnarounds

CHEETAH

Oh, what joy for those
whose disobedience is forgiven,
whose sin is put out of sight!

—PSALM 32:1, NLT

Cheetahs are the fastest land mammals in the world. They've been clocked going from zero to sixty miles per hour in just three seconds! And if a cheetah needs to make a sudden turn while going that fast? No worries! God gave this spotted speedster the perfect tool to make it as agile as it is fast: its tail.

When a cheetah moves its tail one way or the other, the fast feline can quickly change direction, even at full speed. Pretty cool, right?

It's not as easy for us to change direction when we're running at full speed, but God has given us a tool to help us turn around when we go against His instructions. Whenever our thoughts and actions don't match up with God's perfect plans, we have an open invitation to re-direct ourselves toward Him through repentance.

Repentance is the Bible word for changing direction away from sin and toward God's life-giving ways. When we repent, we admit that we did the wrong thing, and we choose to obey God instead. (All with Jesus's help, of course!)

Many people try to avoid repentance because they think admitting they're wrong will make them feel too ashamed. But that isn't God's design! God always loves us, and as soon as we ask, He forgives and renews us. Then God helps us move in the *right* direction with freedom and joy.

So let's start celebrating repentance as the wonderful gift it is. It's such an important part of a healthy, happy life.

Make It Stick }} *Start walking in a certain direction. Then quickly turn around to remind yourself of the gift of repentance.*

Live It Out }} *What do you need to ask God to forgive you for? Don't wait. Confess it now and tell God you're sorry. Receive His forgiveness. Then celebrate His unfailing love!*

Fun Fact
Cheetahs can't roar, but they do purr and chirp.

Soothing the Sting

RHINO

The LORD watches over you—
the LORD is your shade at your right hand.

—PSALM 121:5

Rhinos are one of the largest land animals. They are tough, strong, and fast. But even though their skin is very thick, it's also sensitive to sunburns and insect bites. And when the sun beats down and the bugs chow down, a mud bath is the perfect way for rhinos to get relief and protection. It cools them off, repels ticks and flies, and acts as sunscreen against the sun's powerful rays.

Sometimes we feel tough like the rhino's thick hide. But then there are times when all the difficult things about life add up and we need some relief! Maybe we feel drained from all the struggles. Maybe we feel the bite of unkind words or the sting of disappointment. Just like the rhino seeks out all the soothing benefits of a mud bath, we need to seek out help and protection from God. We can go to Him regularly and experience the refreshment and peace He is longing to give.

So how do we connect with God and experience this kind of care? We can . . .

- Pray and remember God is with us.
- Enjoy nature and remember God made us too.
- Talk with a trustworthy person and remember that God has placed us in a loving community.

- Read a favorite Bible verse and remember how God strengthens us.

- Listen to an encouraging worship song and remember all God has done for us.

Don't wait until the problems of life wear you down. Run to God daily like the rhino runs to its mud bath. Let God cover you and comfort you, refresh you and restore you, protect you and prepare you to face the world again.

Make It Stick *Touch your head. Touch your toes. Imagine God's refreshment and peace covering you all over, inside and out.*

Fun Fact

Rhino horns are primarily made from the same material as our hair and fingernails!

Live It Out *Look at the bulleted list above and choose one way to connect with God this week. Circle it, bookmark it, write yourself a note—whatever it takes to remember to run to God.*

An Amazing Run

GREEN BASILISK LIZARD

Trust GOD from the bottom of your heart;
    don't try to figure out everything on your own.
Listen for GOD's voice in everything you do,
    everywhere you go;
    he's the one who will keep you on track.

—PROVERBS 3:5–6, MSG

The green basilisk lizard can run on top of water! How can it do something so astounding? Its long toes have skin flaps that unfurl to give it more support, and its strong hind legs propel it forward. As its feet slap the water, tiny air pockets form to help keep it afloat. This speedy lizard can stay above water for fifteen feet or more before sinking into a strong swim.

You may know about the time Jesus walked on water. But it wasn't His toes or speed that kept Him above the waves. It was His power as God's Son. When His disciple Peter asked to walk on the water too, Jesus called him out onto the lake. And Peter did it! He walked on the water with Jesus.

Then Peter looked at the strong wind and rough waves and got scared. He doubted and started to sink. But Jesus was there to save him!

Like the basilisk lizard can do what seems impossible, we can do amazing things for God through the power Jesus gives. Every time we stand up for what's right, put others' needs before our own, or give God praise instead of taking compliments for ourselves, we're doing something beyond what's natural. Like walking on water.

Of course, there will be times when we get scared and forget to trust God. But even if we feel like we're sinking in worry or fear, we don't have to be discouraged.

God made a way for basilisks to keep going when they sink. They're great swimmers!

God made a way for Peter to keep going too. Jesus helped him back into the boat!

And God can make a way for us to keep going whatever we face. He never ever leaves us!

Let's remember and celebrate that God gives us power to serve Him. And He picks us up when we fall.

Make It Stick { *Point up and say, "If I'm up . . ." Then point down and say, "If I fall . . ." Then clap your hands and say, "God is with me through it all."*

Live It Out { *Write down one thing you would do for God if you weren't afraid of falling.*

_____

Trust that He's got you and take that next step.

Fun Fact
The basilisk lizard can stay underwater for ten minutes or more without coming up for air.

Connected Community

LACE CORAL

Encourage each other and build each
other up, just as you are already doing.

—1 THESSALONIANS 5:11, NLT

Lace coral, also known as cauliflower coral, isn't food *or* clothing. It's one of the many types of hard corals in our ocean's reefs!

And even though lace coral may look like a rock or a plant, it's made up of many tiny animals. Each coral polyp has a soft body surrounded by a hard skeleton. It sweeps food into its mouth with tentacles and also receives nutrients from algae living inside it.

Lace corals develop together in a colony, but they don't just happen to live side by side. They are *joined* together. A thin layer of tissue called the coenosarc (**see**-nuh-sark) overlays the stony skeleton of the entire colony. This links all the corals, allowing them to share nutrients. It's like having a giant community stomach!

God made His family to be like that too: connected! (But, thankfully, *not* sharing a stomach.) Like corals, followers of Jesus must give and receive to form a healthy community. Some people get in the habit of only giving. When they need help, they don't let anyone know. Other people receive care from others but don't contribute their own gifts and efforts. God's family will thrive only when

we all share back and forth. Worshipping side by side with other believers is a good *start* to a strong Christian family. But being connected is more than that.

One shares a concern. Another prays.

One shares truth. Another receives wisdom.

One shares a need. Another gives what they have.

One shares a celebration. Another rejoices.

One shares a struggle. Another encourages.

One shares talents and gifts. Another gives thanks.

God wants each of us to give and receive, like corals share to keep the whole reef healthy. Then we'll be better able to grow in our faith and show the world God's love.

Make It Stick *Focus on your breath as you take in air and let it out. Like breathing in and out, thank God that we can be strengthened by others' gifts and share our own.*

Live It Out *Let's practice giving help and accepting help this week! Write down one idea for each action and be on the lookout for more opportunities.*

One way I can give help:

_____

One way I can accept help:

_____

Fun Fact
Though it has a delicate name, lace coral is strong, fast growing, and not as sensitive to environmental conditions as some other corals are.

Make a Difference

PECCARY

Our Father in heaven,
your name be honored as holy.
Your kingdom come.
Your will be done
on earth as it is in heaven.

—MATTHEW 6:9–10, csb

Peccaries may not be huge, but these hairy piglike animals make a big difference. Their natural survival strategies actually shape the areas where they live. As they travel around, they tromp down vegetation to make paths other animals use. They also eat fruit and then poop out seeds so new plants can grow.

One of the biggest ways these ecosystem engineers contribute is by wallowing. Scientists have noticed this is especially true for the peccaries in tropical forests. As peccaries roll in the mud to stay cool and remove parasites from their bodies, they leave depressions in the ground. When it rains, the holes fill up with water. And since they are lined with water-resistant clay, molded by peccaries as they wallow, these puddles stay full longer than others, even during the dry season. Many birds, bats, and other beasts rely on this consistent water source. Plus, the peccary-made puddles are great places for frogs and toads to lay their eggs.

Similarly, when we follow God's ways, we can make a huge impact on the people and places around us. Every time we do good, we are making this world a little more like God's original design. We may not always see the outcome of our kindness, patience, and generosity, but God does. And He spreads and multiplies the positive results in ways we could never dream of. He makes us like ecosystem engineers for His kingdom!

When we remember what God's kingdom is like, it gets even more exciting. This is a place where love reigns and selfishness can't be found. Where everyone has enough and everything celebrates God's goodness. Now, that's an awesome place!

Yes, God has good plans, and He wants us to be part of them. So even when it seems as if what we do doesn't make a difference, let's keep following God. When we live as He has taught us, we are making earth a little more like heaven every day.

Make It Stick } *Think about how wonderful God's kingdom is! Then clap, shout, or sing for God.*

Live It Out } *Pray the key verses (MATTHEW 6:9-10) out loud and ask God to show you one way you can help our world be more like His kingdom.*

Fun Fact
When peccaries sense danger, they can make the hair along their spines—their dorsal manes—stand up. They might also clack their teeth together.

Built to Last

SOCIABLE WEAVER

Whatever you do, do it from the heart, as something done for the Lord and not for people, knowing that you will receive the reward of an inheritance from the Lord. You serve the Lord Christ.

—COLOSSIANS 3:23-24, CSB

The sociable weaver may not be the most colorful bird, but its giant nest definitely stands out. Though its home looks like a huge, messy haystack, it's actually a carefully constructed system of passageways and nesting chambers made of dried grasses with a roof of sticks to protect the inside from rain.

For sociable weavers, the work starts before they place a single piece of grass. They must first choose the right spot, usually a smooth tree or pole because of how difficult it is for predators to climb. Even when the nest is complete, the work continues. Since they build with grasses that decay over time, the birds are constantly adding new material to keep their homes strong. This is important because some of them live in the same nest their whole lives. When the original nest builders are gone, their children, grandchildren, and great-grandchildren may continue using the nest. And this can go on for more than a hundred years!

Fun Fact

Sociable weaver nests can house from ten to four hundred birds—and not just sociable weavers. The redheaded finch, African pygmy falcon, and other birds also find refuge from the Kalahari Desert in weaver nests.

It's not always easy to work hard and stay positive about the things we have to do, but the careful, diligent work of the sociable weaver can motivate us to give our best effort. Its enduring nest reminds us that our work can have a positive impact on others beyond what we can see right away. Whether we're taking on chores, schoolwork, or community service, every job—big or small, boring or fun—is a chance to honor the Creator of the universe.

Of course, God looks at more than just the finished product. He also cares about our hearts. He wants us to do our work with a good attitude and give it our all, even

when no one is watching. He wants us to do every job like we're doing it for Him.

Let's remember the huge, strong, long-lasting nest of the sociable weaver and work with happy hearts!

Make It Stick 〉 *Write your name on the badge below. Underneath your name, write, "I work for the Lord." Feel free to decorate with things that remind you of God's love.*

MY NAME IS

Live It Out 〉 *Let's pray!*

Dear God, I really love _____ ,
                                            [job you like]

but I really don't like _____ .
                                        [job you don't like]

Please give me the strength to honor You no matter what I'm working on.

Tougher Than Tough Times

ARAPAIMA

I know what it is to be in need, and I know what it is to have plenty. I have learned the secret of being content in any and every situation, whether well fed or hungry, whether living in plenty or in want. I can do all this through him who gives me strength.

—PHILIPPIANS 4:12–13

The arapaima is a tough fish. Its hard scales are stronger than sharp piranha teeth. It perseveres when the flooded rivers of the Amazon rainforest carry it far from home. And it can live for twenty-four hours on land—completely out of the water!

God made the arapaima able to withstand incredible extremes, and these fish can inspire us when times get tough.

No one wants to go through hard things, but we often underestimate how resilient God has made us. We forget that He can give us strength in new places, difficult times, and scary situations. When we rely on God, we can make it through a lot.

We see this in the life of the apostle Paul. As he traveled around, telling people about the good news of Jesus, he faced some hard times, like being jailed and shipwrecked. He often had to rely on others to give him food, clothing, and shelter. Sometimes there was plenty, and other times there wasn't enough.

But that didn't discourage Paul. He had his mind on God's purposes. It often wasn't easy, but Paul said he learned to be content no matter his circumstances because of the strength Jesus gave him.

Does it feel like you're living among piranhas like the arapaima does? Or does it feel like the floods of life have carried you to an unfamiliar place? Remember, Jesus can give you strength in all kinds of situations. As you trust in the Lord, you can learn to be satisfied whether you have a little or a lot, whether life is calm or chaotic. He will bring you through.

Make It Stick } *Lift your hands in praise and thank God that He is with us when we have plenty. Now hold your hands in front of you, palms facing up like you're waiting to receive something, and thank God that He is with us when we have needs.*

Live It Out } *Think of a struggle you're dealing with. Whisper it to God and ask Him to give you the strength you need.*

Fun Fact

Arapaima dads carry their babies in their mouths to protect them from danger while arapaima moms fight off predators. What a team!

Filter Out and Fill Up!

HUMPBACK WHALE

Brothers and sisters, whatever is true, whatever is noble, whatever is right, whatever is pure, whatever is lovely, whatever is admirable—if anything is excellent or praiseworthy—think about such things.

—PHILIPPIANS 4:8

A lot of animals have teeth. But humpback whales use baleen instead.

What is baleen? Think of long, bristly combs made of the same material as your hair and fingernails. When a whale makes a catch of krill or small fish, salt water and sometimes silt get in its mouth too. The baleen allows the whale to filter out the unwanted stuff and hang on to the healthy meal. Without baleen, the whale would have to swallow a bunch of water and dirt and have less room for the food it needs.

Just like many things come at whales in the ocean, many things come at us each day. Some of them—like kind words and smiles—feed our souls well. Others—like snubs and mean comments—just weigh us down. We may not have baleen to help sort the good from the bad, but we do have the choice not to "swallow" everything we encounter. With God as our guide, we can filter out what's not helpful and keep what's good for us.

The Bible tells us to fill our minds with what is true and pure and lovely (PHILIPPIANS 4:8). Some ways to put this into

practice are to remember a time God helped us, think about our favorite Bible story, or hold on to a kind word from a teacher or friend. We can notice when someone acts in a caring way or speaks up for what's right. We can even recall a beautiful image, like sunlight streaming through our window, or a stunning piece of art. Though they're sometimes easy to overlook, God gives us many excellent things to think about.

It's a gift to filter out discouragement and fill up on what's true! So let's hold on to the promises in God's Word. Let's take in support from those around us. And let's focus on the Holy Spirit whispering, "You are loved."

Fun Fact

When they migrate, humpback whales travel farther than almost any other mammal. They travel up to five thousand miles each year, which is like going across the United States from the Atlantic to the Pacific . . . and back again!

Make It Stick 〉〉 *Think of three good things to fill your mind with.*
They just might be so good that you start to smile!

Live It Out 〉〉 *Pray this prayer:*

Dear excellent and praiseworthy God,
This week, help me notice when I start hanging on to
untrue, negative thoughts so I can filter them out.
Please encourage my heart as I hold on to these true,
lovely thoughts instead:

You made me with love.
You give me strength.
You never ever leave me.

Spread the Good News

HONEYBEE

Give thanks to the LORD and proclaim his greatness.
Let the whole world know what he has done.

—PSALM 105:1, NLT

Honeybees are excellent at spreading good news! When a bee finds a flower's sweet nectar, a great water source, or a perfect place to move the hive, it wants other bees to know. And it shares the news by dancing. The more energetic the dance, the more the other bees realize that the scout bee must have found something *really* good, something worth checking out.

If we are Christians, we've also found something worth sharing: Jesus!

Jesus gives us love, forgiveness, guidance, purpose, and friendship that will last forever. Let's celebrate and spread the word! The Bible has tons of examples of people showing excitement about Jesus.

The disciple Andrew went to tell his brother about Jesus after spending *just one day* with the Lord (JOHN 1:39–41). After Jesus talked with the woman at the well, she told her *whole* town, and many people believed (4:28–39). And when Mary Magdalene realized Jesus had risen from the grave, she *ran* to tell the disciples the wonderful news (MATTHEW 28:5–8). There are so many ways to share our enthusiasm about who Jesus is. (Honeybee dancing isn't required!)

A good place for us to start is by telling about our own relationship with Jesus. We could . . .

- Tell how Jesus answered a prayer or encouraged us.
- Talk about something awesome in God's creation.
- Explain why we love knowing Jesus.

Another way to share is to tell our friends the good news that God cares for *them* too. As we do, let's remember that our friends may have different beliefs than we do. Listening and speaking with respect and kindness is an important way to show them love.

Jesus is sweeter than a flower's nectar is to a honeybee. He forgives us, provides for us, and cares for us. Our excitement about Him can help others seek Him. And a relationship with Jesus is the best gift ever!

Fun Fact

Bees usually try to find food close to home, but they can travel up to five miles away from the hive!

Make It Stick } *In each petal below, write something wonderful about who God is or what He's done for you.*

Live It Out } *Choose an idea from the bulleted list in today's devotion, and be intentional in sharing your excitement about Jesus this week! You could also come up with your own ideas for spreading the word about Jesus's amazing love.*

Stronger with Play

LION

You make known to me the path of life;
you will fill me with joy in your presence,
with eternal pleasures at your right hand.

—PSALM 16:11

God designed young animals to play! And lion cubs are no exception. They wrestle with one another, pounce on Mom, and even use balls of elephant poop like toys.

Play isn't just *enjoyable* for the cubs. It's helpful! During play, lion cubs learn important skills like prowling and chasing. Since they're having fun, little lions end up practicing their survival skills over and over again.

At times, it may seem like faith is all about believing things or doing things. But a very real part of our relationship with God is *enjoying Him.* Just like lion cubs play to grow stronger, we can discover fun ways to grow a strong, joyful relationship with God.

Here are a few ways to enjoy the Lord and add more fun to your faith practices:

- Read your Bible in a favorite place, like a park, backyard tree, or comfy chair.
- Find a new song you like that glorifies God, and play it while you shoot hoops, hang out in your room, or color a picture.
- Take a walk and give God thanks for the things you notice in nature.

- Text favorite Bible verses to a friend or family member.

- Start a prayer journal. You can write out your prayers with your favorite markers or draw pictures of your requests.

- Go on a secret mission with God to do an act of kindness or hide a note of encouragement for someone you know.

- Write your own song, rap, or poem that tells God what's on your mind.

- Tell God something funny that happened during your day, and laugh about it together.

These are just some of the many ways to bring more playfulness into our relationship with the Lord, and if one activity isn't helpful, we can always try another. As we enjoy God more, we won't only have fun—we'll also grow stronger, just like lion cubs.

Make It Stick 〉 *Just for fun, spin around and around. How many things can you thank God for before you get too dizzy?*

Live It Out 〉 *What's one way you'd like to add more play or fun to your time with God this week? Maybe it's something from the list of ideas above!*

Fun Fact
Lions are the only cats known to roar together. And even though lion cubs can't roar yet, they join in with their mews.

Speak Up! Listen Up!

VERVET MONKEY

Dear brothers and sisters, if another believer is overcome by some sin, you who are godly should gently and humbly help that person back onto the right path.

—GALATIANS 6:1, NLT

In the forests and shrublands of Africa, vervet monkeys warn one another about leopards, snakes, eagles, and more. For each predator, they have a different call. These very specific predator alarms can help the monkeys stay safe. Eagle in flight? Look up. Snake in the grass? Look down. Leopard nearby? Go up in the trees!

We also have the power to sound the alarm and help others stay safe when the enemy of our faith comes around. The Bible says the devil is like a prowling predator who wants to destroy God's family of believers (1 PETER 5:8). Like vervets, we can work together to protect one another from the devil's plans. We may not have loud calls, but we do have different ways we can speak up:

- We can help others stay true to God by reminding them of God's good plans and great love for them.
- We can humbly and lovingly talk with other Christians when they do or say things that go against Jesus's life-giving ways.

And it's just as important to listen when other believers do the same for us. We honor God when we open our spiritual ears and respond to truth, encouragement, or warning when we need it.

We want our brothers and sisters in Christ to be far from the devil's lies and destruction. And we want to be far from his schemes ourselves! By staying alert and working together, we can help one another live for the Lord. Like vervets, let's be willing to speak up to protect others. And let's keep our ears open for alarms that can guide *us* safely along God's path too.

Make It Stick } *If you were a wild animal, what kind of sound would you make to warn your family of danger? Practice your sound now (but let the people around you know that everything is fine).*

Live It Out } *Pray this prayer: "Mighty God, please fill me with love and let me use my words well as I encourage other believers to stand strong in their faith. When someone tries to help me back onto the right path, may I be humble enough to listen."*

Fun Fact
Vervet monkeys have cheek pouches, allowing them to stuff food in and save it for later.

Hungry, Hungry, Hungry

WOLVERINE

Blessed are those who hunger and thirst for righteousness, for they will be filled.

—MATTHEW 5:6

Wolverines work hard to eat. They may have to walk miles in a single day just to find food. Sometimes they hunt, but other times they scavenge or dig down deep in the snow to find dead animals that other predators have left. When meat is hard to come by, they look for fruit and seeds to eat.

But wolverines never let a shortage of one kind of food keep them from getting a meal. They are determined. They are resourceful. Because they are hungry. And in more than one way!

Hungry can mean your tummy is rumbling, but it's also a way to say that someone *really* wants something. For example, you can be hungry for a win or hungry for knowledge.

Jesus said it's good for people to be hungry for righteousness. This means wanting the good things of God to fill our hearts, our communities, and our world. Similar to the wolverine's hunger, our hunger for righteousness moves us to do something. The action may be internal, like asking God to help us be more like Jesus, or external, like doing what we can to bring peace, mercy, and truth to whatever situation we're in.

There are lots of things we could want in this world, but hungering for what's right and true will always bless and fill us. It's good for us, and it's good for our world. And we don't have to wait for the perfect circumstance to invite God to work His righteousness in and through us. Hungry people look for every opportunity!

Fun Fact

Wolverine moms give birth and raise their kits in deep snow dens. Though the dens are made of snow, they trap heat and guard the family from windy, frigid weather.

Make It Stick { *Place one hand over your stomach (where you hunger for food) and one over your heart (where you hunger for righteousness). Ask God to give you a strong hunger for what is right and true.*

Live It Out { *In each of the empty spaces on the plate below, write one thing you can do to honor God. Once your plate is full of the righteousness you hunger for, put your plans into action!*

Packed with Power

PEACOCK MANTIS SHRIMP

Don't let anyone look down on you because you are young, but set an example for the believers in speech, in conduct, in love, in faith and in purity.

—1 TIMOTHY 4:12

The colorful peacock mantis shrimp is small. But its powerful punch can bust open crab shells and even break an aquarium's glass—all at a speed that's fifty times faster than we can blink!

A mind-blowing punch isn't the only amazing talent of the peacock mantis shrimp. Its eyes can move in different directions, allowing it to take in two views at once. Plus, it can see a special type of light that spirals. And scientists believe it may be the only animal that can!

It's quite incredible that God put all these abilities in such a tiny package. Did you know that He did a similar thing when He made you?

That's right! God placed special gifts and talents inside you. He planned good ways you can make a difference. And you don't have to be grown-up to start!

Take Timothy from the Bible as an example. Some people thought he was too young to make a difference. But Paul said Timothy's age didn't matter. He could not only live for God but also be an example to other believers.

Maybe you love to draw, sing, garden, or make people laugh. Maybe you're good at noticing things in nature or sharing kind words. Each amazing attribute God gave you can become a way to help and encourage others. Just like He packed the tiny peacock mantis shrimp with some big abilities, He has placed wonderful gifts inside you. And He put you in just the right spot to start making a difference.

God can make you an inspiration to others and an example of His grace, whatever your age or size. Ask Him to help you live so that others see His power in you.

Make It Stick 〉 Grab a sheet of paper (or use the blank space below) and draw a picture of yourself. Then around your drawing, write or draw some of the gifts and talents God has planted inside you.

Live It Out 〉 Read our key verse (1 TIMOTHY 4:12) and circle one way you want to be an example this week: in how you talk, in how you act, in how you love others . . . There are so many ways to live for God!

Incredible Restoration

OCTOPUS

I have told you these things, so that in me you may have peace. In this world you will have trouble. But take heart! I have overcome the world.

—JOHN 16:33

The octopus is an amazing creature. It has three hearts, nine brains (one of which is shaped like a doughnut!), and blue blood. Plus, it's super smart and a master of camouflage.

Something else that's pretty incredible about the octopus? If it loses an arm, it can grow another one that's just as strong as the first! This restoration takes a significant amount of time—about 130 days from start to finish.

Sometimes *we* face losses too. Some losses, like missing a party or losing a toy, make us sad for a little while. Others are things we'll always miss, like a family member who passes away or a friend who moves. These difficult situations can really hurt our hearts. We may even feel like part of us is missing. But God is there to heal our broken hearts, just like He restores the octopus's arm.

God's heart-healing process may take time, but He gives us many gifts as we wait:

- **PRAYER:** Talk with God about your sadness. He understands and He cares.
- **PROCESS:** Work out your big feelings by getting active, doing creative projects, or going on a walk.

- **PEOPLE:** Talk with a family member, friend, teacher, or counselor about your emotions.

- **PRACTICE:** Be on the lookout for a friend's smile, the beauty of nature, or another hint of God's love. God is always with us and sends us reminders of His presence.

- **PROMISES:** The Bible is full of comfort and hope, including God's promise that in heaven, there will be no more crying or pain (REVELATION 21:4).

When you experience a loss, however big or small, go to the Lord. He is waiting to heal your heart.

Fun Fact

The octopus can camouflage in the blink of an eye. It changes not only its color but also its pattern, texture, shape, and behavior to blend into its environment or mimic other animals.

Make It Stick

Connect the dotted lines to make the heart whole. Thank God that He has the power to comfort us and heal what's broken.

Live
It
Out Look at the list above. Circle the gift that you want to try the next time you're facing a loss or disappointment. Whatever the size or the situation, God is with us in our sadness.

Love That Won't Give Up

SALMON

I give you a new command: Love each other deeply and fully. Remember the ways that I have loved you, and demonstrate your love for others in those same ways.

—JOHN 13:34, VOICE

When it's time for salmon to lay eggs, they go back to the stream, river, or lake where they were born. They swim for miles against the current, which is like going the wrong way on an escalator or moving sidewalk. All the while, predators such as bears and eagles are trying to gobble them up. To overcome waterfalls and other obstacles, salmon may jump higher than an Olympic athlete. Then they carefully make a nest, bury their eggs, and guard them. This whole journey can take six months, and most of them do it without eating a thing!

Salmon sacrifice so much for their eggs. Their determination can inspire us to follow one of God's most important commands: "Love your neighbor as yourself" (MARK 12:31).

Sometimes, loving other people is fun and joyful. Sometimes it's really hard—harder than swimming upstream and jumping up a waterfall! Showing love can be especially difficult when it means doing things we don't want to do. But like the salmon swims against the natural flow of the river, God can give us the strength to do the opposite of our own desires.

Our ultimate example of sacrificial love is Jesus. He came from heaven to earth to show us God's love, even dying on the cross. And He continues to show us generous, unselfish love every day. Jesus is a friend who never fails.

The next time one of your relationships seems difficult, don't give up! Remember the salmon's determination. And most important, remember Jesus's sacrificial love for you. Focusing on how He loves you will help you love others well.

Make It Stick 〉 *Jump as high as you can, like a salmon jumping up a waterfall. As you jump, thank God that He can fuel your words, thoughts, and actions to help you show love to others—even when it's hard.*

Live It Out 〉 *What has been your most difficult relationship lately? Ask God what you can do to show love to that person.*

Fun Fact

Salmon are one of the few types of fish that can live in both salt water and fresh water. They are born in fresh water, feed in the salty ocean water, and then go back to fresh water.

Maximize
the Light

C A T

Oh, how I love your law!
I meditate on it all day long.

—PSALM 119:97

Have you ever seen a cat's eyes glowing at night?

God gave cats a special way to see better in the dark. They have a structure at the back of the eye called the tapetum lucidum (tuh-**pee**-tum **loo**-sih-dum). The tapetum lucidum is like a mirror that reflects light back into the eye to produce a brighter image. By reflecting the light, the tapetum lucidum gives the cat's eye another chance to absorb the light it needs to see clearly. And this is similar to what happens when we meditate on God's Word!

Meditating on God's Word is more than just reading or listening to the Bible. When we meditate on a Bible verse, we let it come back into our minds a second time—or many times. We really think about the meaning of the verse. We sense the emotion behind it. We get curious about its purpose. We stay with it a bit longer to give ourselves a better chance of absorbing the goodness it holds and understanding what it means for our lives.

Let's look at some ways we can let God's Word sink into our hearts and minds:

- Read it again.
- Read it aloud.

- Touch each word as you read.

- Listen to it on a Bible app.

- Pick a word or phrase that stands out to you and think about its meaning.

- Ask the Holy Spirit how this verse can make a difference in your life.

- Write the verse and think about each word as you write.

- Illustrate the verse.

- Make up hand motions that represent the verse.

- Change your posture as you read (kneeling, standing, or raising your hands).

No matter how you do it, find ways to reflect on and absorb God's Word. Like the tapetum lucidum helps the cat maximize the light, meditation can help us receive even more wisdom and encouragement from the Bible.

Fun Fact
Cats seem to view a slow blink as a friendly form of communication. If you look a cat in the eye and blink very slowly, it may even return the blink.

Make It Stick   Breathe in and say, "I soak in God's Word . . ."
Breathe out and say, ". . . when I stick with
God's Word."

Live It Out   Let's start now! This week, choose three ways to
meditate on our key verse (PSALM 119:97).

Clever Camouflage

DECORATOR CRAB

As God's chosen people, holy and dearly loved, clothe yourselves with compassion, kindness, humility, gentleness and patience.

—COLOSSIANS 3:12

Decorator crabs do *not* like plain shells. They find sponges, seaweed, and anemones and stick them all over themselves. Curved bristles on the crabs' shells help with that task, acting like Velcro to hold the decorations tight.

As you may have guessed, the crabs are doing more than expressing their personal style. They're also camouflaging themselves to blend into their environment and stay safe from predators.

You may be wondering what camouflage has to do with being a Christian. After all, Jesus wants us to shine for Him, tell others about Him, and not be ashamed of Him. No camouflage there!

But Jesus also said not to do good deeds to try to get attention and praise. It's better to serve quietly to honor God than loudly to get honor for ourselves.

Back in Jesus's day (and all throughout history), people did good deeds to show off. They prayed and gave money to people in need just so others would admire them. But

Jesus said that good deeds aren't for getting compliments. Our good works should come from a true desire to help others because we're grateful for all God has done for us.

Serving to get attention is all wrapped up in pride—thinking we're better than others. And pride is as dangerous to the human heart as a hungry octopus is to the decorator crab! So, like the decorator crab dresses up to blend in, we can clothe ourselves in humility and avoid the predator of pride.

When we do kind things for others, let's serve with sincere and humble hearts. If someone does notice, we can share that Jesus is the source of the love inside us and point all the praise toward Him.

Make It Stick *Say the key verse (COLOSSIANS 3:12) out loud and pretend you're getting dressed in the godly clothing it describes.*

Live It Out *Think up a secret way to serve someone this week, and make a plan to do it. Have fun with it!*

Fun Fact
Decorator crabs are excellent at recycling! When it's time for them to shed their old shells, they reuse the decorations on their new shells.

Expert Navigation

NARWHAL

Listen to advice and accept instruction,
that you may gain wisdom in the future.

—PROVERBS 19:20, ESV

Have you ever heard your echo? It's fun when your voice bounces back to you, but animals don't use echoes for fun. They use them to understand their environment and locate prey. This is called echolocation. Bats are well known for their echolocation ability, but narwhals may be the best at it.

Narwhals send out clicks—up to one thousand per second—through their foreheads. They can expertly focus the clicks on smaller or larger areas. The clicks bounce off objects and send sound waves back to the narwhals, giving them the precise information they need to navigate around obstacles and find food in the dark arctic waters.

Because God gave them the perfect tool, it would be

silly (and harmful) if narwhals didn't use echolocation and just went bumping into ice or charging to the depths with no direction.

But sometimes that's exactly what *we* do! We try to navigate life blindly instead of using two important tools: God's Word and prayer. Since God is the author of life, when we go to Him in prayer and read the Bible, we can better understand the world and His plan for us in it. The more time we spend with Him, the more we know how to get around obstacles and find our way.

Another resource God gave to help us set a good course is people. By asking questions of trustworthy people and listening to their advice, we are being just like the narwhal—sending out clicks and receiving back a signal. However, we should still bring that advice back to God and ask Him how we can use it in our lives, as He's always the best guide.

Don't wander around in the dark. Instead, think like a narwhal! Seek out the direction you need to navigate life.

Fun Fact

The narwhal tusk is actually a tooth. The upper left canine tooth grows through the narwhal's lip to form a spiral tusk. In very rare cases, a narwhal can grow two tusks.

Make It Stick Grab a pencil and paper and try drawing a narwhal with your eyes closed. Then open your eyes and try again. As you look at your two pictures, thank God that we can see life more clearly when we gain wisdom from Him and the people around us.

Live It Out Write down the names of a few people in your life who love God and are trying to live for Him. The next time you need advice or have a question, ask one of them for wisdom.

_____

_____

Soar with Hope

GOLDEN EAGLE

Those who hope in the LORD
will renew their strength.
They will soar on wings like eagles;
they will run and not grow weary,
they will walk and not be faint.

—ISAIAH 40:31

Eagles can fly for a long time without flapping their wings. And one type that loves to soar is the golden eagle.

These birds are skilled at finding columns of rising air, or updrafts, that can lift them more than fifteen thousand feet in the air. When eagles catch an updraft, they start soaring in circles and then glide out over the land. To stay steady, they keep their wings outstretched and use small muscles to adjust to the wind's movement. By allowing the wind to lift them, eagles get a break from constantly flapping. In fact, golden eagles spend just 15 percent or less of their flight time flapping. That's a lot of soaring!

Just like eagles rely on the wind currents to rise to amazing heights, we can rely on the Holy Spirit to lift us and carry us. We get worn-out when we try to fly through life on our own and forget to trust God.

But we get a completely different result when we put our hope in the Lord. Our God is steady, everlasting, and powerful. When we believe His promises and trust Him to help, He renews our strength and gives us peace. Then our hearts can rest and our spirits can soar, knowing He is always faithful.

What a beautiful picture of how God strengthens us with hope!

Everyone gets tired sometimes. Everyone stumbles. But those who look to the Lord and expect Him to show up renew their strength. They soar! They glide! They take comfort in their Creator, whose love and power never fail.

Make It Stick *Stretch out your arms as far as they can go, and pretend to soar around like an eagle. Imagine that God is lifting you higher and higher, and trust Him to fill you with strength.*

Live It Out *What's weighing you down? Write it in the blank and give it to God as you say the prayer below. It's based on our key verse (ISAIAH 40:31).*

Lord, You say that when I count on You about

_____ , You will renew my

strength. Thank You for promising to help me soar

like an eagle.

Take the Leap!

GIBBON

Don't hesitate to be enthusiastic—be on fire in the Spirit as you serve the Lord! Be happy in your hope, stand your ground when you're in trouble, and devote yourselves to prayer.

—ROMANS 12:11-12, CEB

Gibbons swing from branch to branch two hundred feet above the rainforest floor. It may shock you to learn that—even from that height—sometimes they fall on purpose, then grab another branch before they plummet all the way to the ground!

But why take the risk of falling in the first place? Scientists think it's all part of the gibbons' quest to become amazing swingers, ready to face any situation. By learning to catch themselves when things are calm, gibbons practice the skills they will need in case a branch unexpectedly breaks.

Practice prepares us for what lies ahead. But it can still feel risky—even if we're not swinging in the treetops—because whenever we try new things, we're not quite sure how they will go. This can be true in our walk with Jesus too. We may feel nervous to try new things in our faith, like praying out loud, telling others about Jesus, or asking questions about God.

Fun Fact
Gibbon calls are long and loud. Male and female gibbons will often call together to strengthen family bonds—each "singing" a different part in a powerful duet.

But don't worry! God isn't grading us. When we take new steps in our faith, it's not about performance; it's about trusting God to help us grow.

With our faith in God, we can be as relaxed and playful as a gibbon when we take new steps (or leaps). And similarly to the way gibbons get support from their family groups, we may find that trying new things is easier when we're with people who care.

Our bravery can encourage others too. Maybe someone else is also afraid to share their questions with the group or read Scripture out loud. But when they see you do it, they gain courage to give it a try.

New things may feel uncomfortable at first, but we can't grow unless we practice. Stay brave, stay playful, give yourself grace, and rely on God. Don't let being new at something stop you. Growing closer to God is always worth it!

Make It Stick *Jump as far as you can across the room and say, "God is with me when I try new things!"*

Live It Out *What is one way you can "take a leap" and grow in your faith? Maybe it's to pray with someone, share about your faith in Jesus, or ask a question in church. Write down the idea you came up with. Don't stress! Instead, think about the playful, practicing gibbon and give it a try.*

_____

_____

An Eye for Gratitude

OWL

Give thanks to the LORD, for he is good;
his love endures forever.

—PSALM 107:1

Y̶ou may know that owls can see well at night, but what's their secret?

Their great night vision starts with their huge eyes! That's how they can take in light, even on really dark nights. And the more light that comes in, the more clearly they see. Owl eyes are not just large. They are also equipped with tons of light-sensing rods and a mirrorlike structure (called *tapetum lucidum*) that reflects light back into the eye and helps them process it in the best way possible.

Amazing eyes help owls see where to go and find what they need. In fact, some owls see a hundred times better than humans can in the dark!

Like owls can see with the tiniest bits of light, we have a surprising way to see when life gets difficult and we feel like we're in the dark. God tells us to give thanks. That doesn't mean we need to be happy about the struggles we're facing, but even in challenging times, there are things to be grateful for.

Fun Fact

Owl eyes are equipped with nictitating membranes, which are like third eyelids that can close to keep debris out while still letting light in.

Giving God thanks for the blessings in our lives helps us take in more light and use it well, just like the owl. Gratitude helps us remember that, even in the middle of really hard situations, we're not alone. Then we can see more clearly, let God guide us, and hold on to His truth. But gratitude doesn't help us only in struggles. In happy times, giving God thanks actually increases our happiness. No matter what, gratitude keeps our hearts open to His reassuring presence.

Our God is always with us. Let's find reasons to give Him thanks and take in the light of His love, even when we're walking through the dark.

Make It Stick 〉 If you can, go to your closet or another dark space. Notice how the longer you're in the dark, the better you can see. As your eyes let in more light and become more sensitive to it, you begin to notice the things that have been there all along. That's exactly how gratitude works!

Live It Out 〉 Grab a sheet of paper (or use the blank space below), set a timer for one minute, and write or draw some things you're grateful for—as many as you can. Each day for the rest of the week, challenge yourself to add three things you haven't already listed.

Help from the Heart

MOUSE (AND RAT!)

All of you, be like-minded, be sympathetic, love one another, be compassionate and humble.

—1 PETER 3:8

"As quiet as a mouse" is a phrase you may have heard before. But it would also be fitting to say, "As caring as a mouse."

Check out what scientists have learned: When a mouse sees another mouse hurt or in trouble, it can sense the other mouse's emotions and experience those same emotions itself. This is true for rats too! But mice and rats don't stop there. Often these rodents do more than just feel for the animal in distress; they do something to help. Rats have even been known to risk their own food to help another rat.

When we try to sense other people's feelings and imagine their point of view, that's called empathy. When we add a desire to help, that's called compassion. Empathy and compassion can move us to truly care for others the way God designed.

Is someone you know going through a tough time? Try to imagine how they're feeling. Then respond with an act of kindness. Could you invite them

Fun Fact

Like birds, mice often sing to attract a mate. The notes are too high for humans to hear, but special microphones can record the songs and play them back in a lower range.

to join you for a fun activity or sit with you at lunch? Could you help them or compliment their work? Maybe they just need you to be a good listener!

It's not always easy to notice others and show we care. But the more we practice empathy and reach out in compassion, the more natural it becomes. We can also look to the wonderful example we have in Jesus. While He was on earth, He not only helped people but also cried with them and rejoiced with them.

Let's ask God to help us see who around us needs empathy and compassion. Then let's love like Jesus.

Make It Stick

"Walk in someone else's shoes" is a way to say, "Imagine someone else's struggles or point of view." In the shoe below, write the names of two or three people God may want you to show empathy and compassion to.

Live It Out

You wrote down some names, right? Now go out and show empathy and compassion to the people you listed. Plan one thing you can say to or do for each of them. If you're struggling to think of something, ask God to guide you!

Meaningful Moments

ELEPHANT

There is a time for everything,
and a season for every activity under the heavens: . . .
a time to weep and a time to laugh,
a time to mourn and a time to dance.

—ECCLESIASTES 3:1, 4

Elephants take time for life's important moments. When an elephant baby is born, all the aunties (other female elephants) gather around and trumpet with their trunks. When an elephant dies, other elephants touch the body and sometimes places leaves or clumps of grass on top of it. At an elephant reunion, ears flap, voices bellow, and trunks intertwine.

God designed *us* to express our joy and sorrow in community too. He knows taking time to celebrate and mourn is important.

But what if we don't take time for these healthy responses? What if good things happen but we don't smile or say thanks? Instead, we barely notice. What if hard things happen but we ignore our needs or stuff down our feelings? We forget God is there to heal our hearts.

That's not God's design. God wants us to fully live! He wants us to know He cares for our souls. Pausing to remember that He is with us in all life's

Fun Fact

Elephant trunks have no bones! They are mostly muscle, and elephants use them for so many things, including smelling, snorkeling, picking up food, and squirting water into their mouths or onto their backs.

moments brings us through the ups and downs with grace and peace.

We see examples of this in the Bible too. When God parted the Red Sea, Moses and his sister, Miriam, led the Israelites to celebrate with singing and dancing (EXODUS 15:1–21). David mourned openly when his best friend, Jonathan, died in battle (2 SAMUEL 1:17–27). When Jesus was born,

His mother, Mary, quietly treasured all the wonderful things that were happening (LUKE 2:13–19).

Elephants remind us to take time for what matters—and not just the big things like births, deaths, and reunions. Answers to prayer and unexpected blessings are opportunities to give thanks and celebrate. Difficult relationships and everyday struggles are reasons to let God and other believers help us work through our feelings. It's healthy to tend to ourselves and our communities, just as our good God planned.

Make It Stick
Stand in front of a mirror and make the following faces, one at a time:

- *Happy*
- *Sad*
- *Surprised*

- *Afraid*
- *Angry*
- *Peaceful*

Say this prayer out loud: "God, thank You for being with me in every season. Help me take time to bring my thoughts and feelings to You."

Live It Out
Be on the lookout this week for opportunities to celebrate, chances to help someone through a difficult situation, and times to acknowledge your own ups and downs. Pause and remember that God is with you in all of life's moments.

Be Wise— Store Up!

ACORN WOODPECKER

Happy are those who find wisdom
and those who gain understanding.

—PROVERBS 3:13, CEB

Acorn woodpeckers make sure they're always prepared! They drill thousands of holes in trees to store acorns for the winter. And they can drill up to fifty thousand hiding spots in just one tree! These birds spend a lot of time guarding the acorn-filled trees from other birds and squirrels. As the acorns dry up and shrink a little, the woodpeckers move them around to different holes, ensuring a perfect fit for every tiny treasure.

This storage practice helps acorn woodpeckers survive when food is hard to come by. If they've stored enough of the tasty treats and protected their stash from other hungry creatures, they won't have to deal with the dangers of migrating somewhere else to find food. They'll have plenty to survive and thrive right at home!

As humans, we also need to make sure we store up and protect a special stash. But not of acorns! What we need is an abundance of wisdom.

We can get that wisdom from the Bible. Its instructions are not limited to the big stuff, like loving God and loving

others—it also shows us the best ways to live. Here are some examples of the insight and knowledge we can get from God's Word:

· The rewards of honesty

· The benefits of controlling our anger

· How to do well at our chores or schoolwork

· The importance of saving, giving, and spending our money well

Like the acorn woodpecker who wisely stores food for the winter, we can gather and treasure the understanding we need for life. If we start tucking away God's wisdom, we'll be more prepared to make wise choices with our words, our money, our time, our relationships, and so much more—now and in the future.

Make It Stick } *Tap your head, put your hands over your heart, and clap your hands. Remember, we need God's wisdom in our minds, hearts, and actions.*

Live It Out } *One way to hold on to the Bible's wisdom is to memorize Scripture. Write today's key verse (PROVERBS 3:13) on a piece of paper or sticky note and put it where you'll see it every day. Try to memorize the verse by the end of the week!*

Plunge In and Practice

BROWN PELICAN

Practice these things, immerse yourself in
them, so that all may see your progress.

—1 TIMOTHY 4:15, ESV

All types of pelicans use their famous throat pouches to
catch fish. But only one species—the brown pelican—does
a high-speed dive from as high as sixty feet in the air to
capture its meal.

How does a brown pelican plunge into the water from
that height without hurting itself? Several pelican parts
work together in this incredible fishing technique:

- Its neck stretches out and muscles tense to protect
  its spine.

- Air pockets fill to cushion other delicate body parts.

- Its spear-like beak pierces the water at just the right angle.

Even though God thoroughly equipped the brown pelican for this death-defying feat, it doesn't catch a fish every time. It still has to work at it, especially if it doesn't have a lot of diving experience yet.

God also equips us for special purposes, but similar to the pelican, just because we were made for something doesn't mean we won't have to work at it.

We could say this the other way too: Just because we have to work at something doesn't mean we weren't made for it. That's what Paul was telling his young friend Timothy in today's verse (1 TIMOTHY 4:15).

When we're trying to improve at something, the word *yet* can be very helpful. Instead of saying, "I can't do that," we can say, "I can't do that *yet*." This reminds us God is still working on us, which gives us the hope and determination to keep going.

As you set out to discover and do what God has designed you for, don't get discouraged. Work at it, celebrate your journey, and keep following Jesus!

Make It Stick } Let's practice using the word yet. Fill in the blanks:

I can't _____ yet.

I can't _____ yet.

I can't _____ yet.

Live It Out } Repeat this prayer every day this week:

Dear God,

Thank You for giving me gifts and talents and skills.

Even though I am struggling with _____,

I will trust You to help me get better because I know

You have good plans for me!

Be a Kid!
Stay a Kid!

AXOLOTL

He said to them, "Let the little children come to me, and do not hinder them, for the kingdom of God belongs to such as these."

—MARK 10:14

Almost all amphibians go through a process called metamorphosis, which is when they change from swimming-in-water creatures that breathe through gills to walking-on-land creatures that breathe through lungs. But one amphibian that doesn't is the axolotl!

Even though an axolotl *does* grow in size and even develops small lungs, it keeps its gills and always lives in the water. This makes the axolotl an amazing creature because it keeps its youthful characteristics its whole life.

In the Bible, Jesus pointed out something equally surprising: Even though God wants us to grow up, there are some ways He wants us to stay young! When people were bringing their little children to Jesus, the disciples said no. But Jesus said yes. He wanted to bless the children. He loved them. He also wanted to point to the children as examples for the adults.

Have you ever seen a small child experience something for the first time, like the taste of ice cream or the beauty of a rainbow? They're so excited and full of amazement! Have you ever seen them run to their

Fun Fact

If axolotls ever get injured, they can grow back their legs, their tails, and even parts of their hearts and brains!

parents after a scare or a fall? They're so trusting! Jesus said God's kingdom belongs to people who are like those children.

So how can we stay like children even as we grow? God wants us to keep our sense of wonder and excitement about Him. He wants us to remember how amazing He is and believe Him when He says, "I love you." God wants us to run to Him when we're happy or sad. He wants us to

enjoy being with Him and soak up all the goodness and love He gives.

When it comes to our faith in the Lord, we should stay youthful like the amazing axolotl. Let's keep trusting Jesus and enjoying Him all the days of our lives.

Make It Stick *Make a silly face or strike a wild pose, and thank God that He made you to enjoy Him at every age. Being a kid is amazing and special—don't ever forget that!*

Live It Out *Let's renew our childlike sense of wonder about God and His creation! Think of a miracle from the Bible or of something beautiful in nature. Draw or write it in the starburst below and decorate all around it as you give thanks to God for how awesome He is.*

A Slow and Peaceful Pace

SLOTH

Come to me, all you who are weary and burdened, and I will give you rest. Take my yoke upon you and learn from me, for I am gentle and humble in heart, and you will find rest for your souls. For my yoke is easy and my burden is light.

—MATTHEW 11:28-30

Sloths are the world's slowest mammals. In a whole day, they don't even travel half the length of a football field!

But we shouldn't let the sloth's name and slow speed give it a bad reputation. Sloths aren't lazy. They just know how to make the most of the energy they have. Because of what they eat and how long it takes them to digest their food, moving *slowly* is just the right speed for a sloth.

We humans can go at different speeds based on the situations we're in. It's always wise to ask ourselves if we're moving at the right pace. Sometimes going fast is best, but not all the time. Jesus was known for reminding people to slow down and focus on what's important.

In our world, many people hurry and scurry about to get the most money they can, the most things they can, the most entertainment they can. It's easy to stay distracted by our goals, activities, screens, and worries. But our bodies and our souls weren't meant to go at such a rushed pace.

We need rest. We need time with Jesus. God wants us to make space in our lives for these important things. When busy times do happen, we can continue to stay in touch with God by talking with Him and focusing on His love. We never want to go so fast that we forget about the Lord.

So let's ask Him to help us go at the right pace, just like the sloth does. Today is a great day to slow down and connect with Jesus.

Make It Stick *Relax your body and take a slow, deep breath. Thank God that He's designed us for a peaceful, healthy pace.*

Live It Out *Ask your parents to help you set an alarm to go off once a day this week so the whole family can pause to pray and remember the restful pace of Jesus.*

Fun Fact
Sloths spend up to 90 percent of their lives upside down. They can eat, sleep, and even give birth this way.

Courageous Climb

ROCK-CLIMBING GOBY

Let us run with perseverance the race marked out for us, fixing our eyes on Jesus, the pioneer and perfecter of faith. For the joy set before him he endured the cross . . . and sat down at the right hand of the throne of God.

—HEBREWS 12:1-2

The rock-climbing gobies of Hawaii can climb straight up waterfalls! As the water crashes down on them, they either use their suction-cup mouths and fins to keep climbing or they simply use their tails to propel themselves upward. But no matter what, these fish are going up—sometimes nearly one thousand feet. That's higher than a seventy-story building!

The journey of faith can be a bit like climbing a waterfall. Sometimes we don't have clear answers to life's tough questions. Other times we must face people being unkind or making fun of us because of what we believe. But all through the Bible, God has given His followers encouragement and examples to help us persevere through difficulties and stand strong in our faith.

In fact, HEBREWS 11:1–12:3 is a power-packed summary of people of faith who never gave up. And the passage ends with the supreme example for us to follow: Jesus.

He left heaven to come to earth, die on the cross, and rise again so that we could fully experience God's love forever. And what kept Him going when He was mocked and persecuted? When He was betrayed and His friends let Him down?

And what about when He was beaten and crucified?

He focused on joy! The joy of rescuing people from sin and death. The joy of obeying His Father. The joy of being with us for all eternity.

Yes, living a life of faith isn't always easy. But God can give us the strength to persevere. We can remember the people of faith who have gone before us, the Savior who is with us, and the joy that awaits us. And—if it helps—we can think of the amazing rock-climbing goby too.

Fun Fact

The Nopoli rock-climbing goby is not the highest climbing of all the goby species, but it has an awesome ability. Before it starts its epic journey, the fish's suction-cup mouth moves closer to its belly to help it climb.

Make It Stick ⦃ Grab a sheet of paper (or use the space below) and draw a waterfall. All around it, write the names of people and other blessings that encourage you in your faith.

Live It Out ⦃ Pray this prayer: "Lord, it's not always easy to follow You in this world. Thank You that You understand. Help me stay strong and keep going as I focus on the joy You give!"

Friendly and Faithful

DOG

Yes indeed, it is good when you obey the royal law as found in the Scriptures: "Love your neighbor as yourself."

—JAMES 2:8, NLT

Those big understanding eyes. That happy wagging tail. Even that excited drooling mouth. Dogs are so friendly that they're called "man's best friend."

But have you ever stopped to wonder how these canine creatures got that nickname? Scientists have! Let's look at a few things they've studied in dogs:

- Dogs seem to understand how we feel. They use our facial expressions, our tone of voice, and even our smell to figure out our emotions.

- Dogs get excited to see us. And when we see their excitement, it usually creates positive feelings in us too.

- Dogs are helpers. You may have heard of dogs pulling sleds in the snow, guiding people who are blind, and sniffing out clues. But scientists have found that even a dog's presence can help us relax and enjoy life.

- Dogs are loyal. They've been known to rescue their owners, wait for them for days, and stick around to cheer them up.

These doggy traits can inspire us to be the kind of friend God wants *us* to be too!

- Good human friends pay attention to others' feelings. Sensing when our friends are excited, happy, sad, or afraid helps us support them in just the right way.
- Good friends also enthusiastically welcome people and make sure they know they matter.
- Good friends find ways to help, even when it's not convenient for them.

Fun Fact

Most people know that dogs have great sniffers. But dogs use their noses for more than smelling! They sense heat using the skin around their nostrils, known as the rhinarium.

- Good friends are loyal. When someone has a bad day, gets teased, or makes a mistake, we can be there to support them, stand up for them, or forgive them. (Of course, if someone is hurting you or telling you to keep something dangerous a secret, that isn't the time to be loyal. Tell someone who can help.)

Jesus said loving others is so important that the only thing that ranks higher is loving God (MATTHEW 22:37–39). So when it comes to friendship, let's follow the example of our furry friends and give it our all!

Make It Stick 〉 *Thank God for friendship as you fill in the blanks from our key verse:*

Love your _____ as _____ .
(JAMES 2:8, NLT)

Live It Out 〉 *Think of someone who needs a friend. Then look at the ideas above. What's one way you can reach out to that person?*

Can't Stop Growing!

RED KANGAROO

We continually ask God to fill you with the knowledge of
his will through all the wisdom and understanding that the
Spirit gives, so that you may live a life worthy of the Lord
and please him in every way: . . . growing in the knowledge
of God . . . and giving joyful thanks to the Father.

—COLOSSIANS 1:9–10, 12

Red kangaroos grab our attention for many reasons.
Kangaroos are the only large mammal to use jumping as
their primary way to move around, and a red kangaroo's
strong legs can propel them twenty-five feet in just
one leap.

But kangaroos stand out among mammals for another

reason. They never stop growing! When they're born, they're only one inch long—about the size of a jelly bean. But red kangaroos can get up to six and a half feet tall. Unlike humans, who reach their maximum height by about age twenty, the kangaroo's skeleton gets bigger all through adulthood.

Though our bodies *will* stop growing one day, our spirits don't have to. When we pray, serve, read the Bible, and share about Jesus, the Lord works in our hearts and helps us grow spiritually.

We can't see spiritual growth the same way we can measure our

height. But we can engage in growth practices like the ones listed above and even things like intentionally taking in God's love and trying to see people the way He does. And as we walk with Him, we can trust that He is helping us develop and mature. Over time, we'll see evidence of our progress as our thoughts, speech, and actions become more like Jesus.

And we don't have to stop! God is so incredible that we'll never say, "I've already learned everything about God, and I've run out of ways to grow." No way! Even when

we've been following Jesus for a long time, there will *still* be so many ways to enjoy God, learn from the Holy Spirit, and demonstrate the love of our Savior.

The red kangaroo reminds us we can keep growing in God—forever! So let's spend time with Him every day and do the good works He's planned for us. Even if we live for a thousand years, we'll never run out of things to love about God.

Make It Stick *Are you curious about how tall you are right now? Ask an adult or a sibling to help you measure yourself. Thank the Lord that He helps us grow, physically and spiritually.*

Live It Out *Growth usually happens little by little. Sometimes we don't even notice it while it's happening. What's one small thing you can do to grow spiritually this week? Write it down and ask God to help you.*

Fun Fact
Kangaroos are great swimmers!

Certificate of

Awesome Animal Expertise

NAME

_____ , _____

DATE

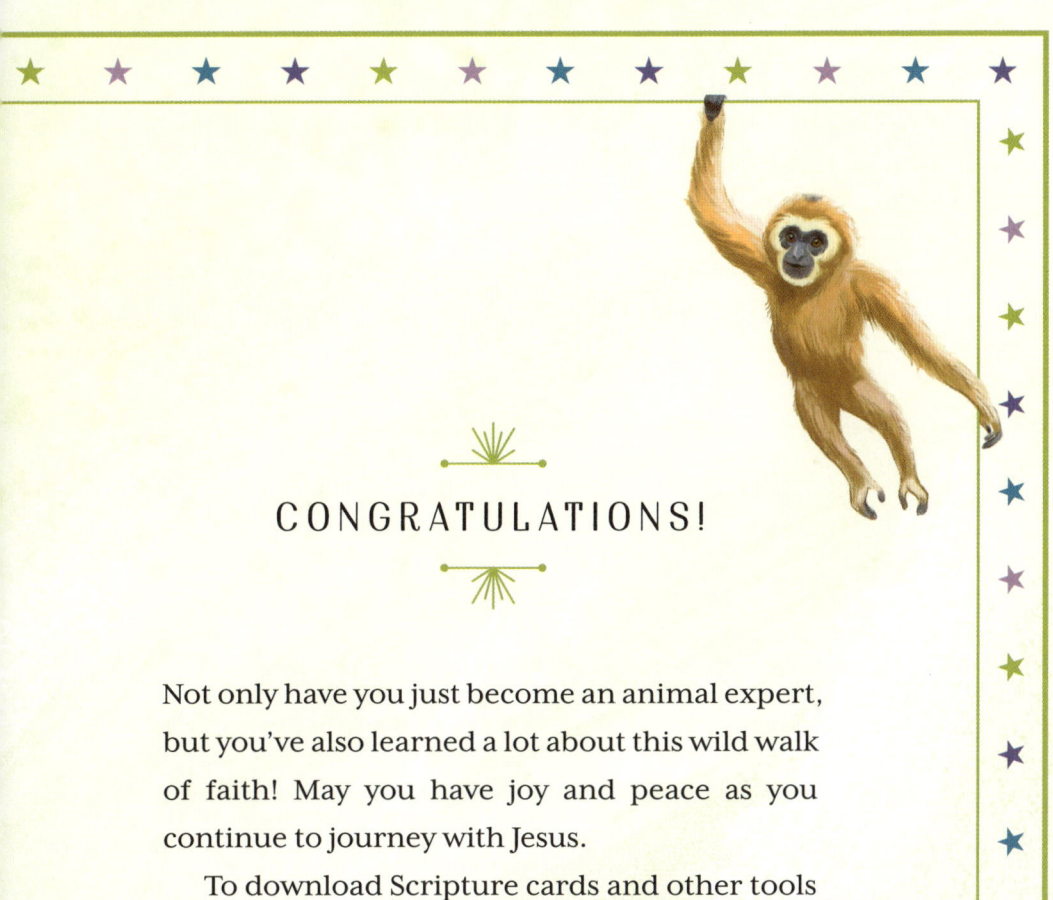

CONGRATULATIONS!

Not only have you just become an animal expert, but you've also learned a lot about this wild walk of faith! May you have joy and peace as you continue to journey with Jesus.

To download Scripture cards and other tools to help you carry what you've learned with you (and learn more about the research behind this book), visit https://valerieellis.com/wildfaith. You can also go through this devotional again or revisit your favorite animal lessons to keep God's truth fresh in your mind and in your heart!

WATERBROOK

An imprint of the Penguin Random House Christian Publishing Group,
a division of Penguin Random House LLC
1745 Broadway, New York, NY 10019
waterbrookmultnomah.com
penguinrandomhouse.com

Note: While the facts provided within this book were valid at the time of publication, please be aware that as new scientific research is verified, some of the details may not reflect the latest findings.

Hardcover ISBN 978-0-593-58259-6
Ebook ISBN 978-0-593-58260-2

The Library of Congress catalog record is available at http://lccn.loc.gov/2025011613.

Printed in China

9 8 7 6 5 4 3 2 1

First Edition

The authorized representative in the EU for product safety and compliance is Penguin Random House Ireland, Morrison Chambers, 32 Nassau Street, Dublin D02 YH68, Ireland. https://eu-contact.penguin.ie

BOOK TEAM: Editor: Bunmi Ishola • Production editor: Jessica Choi • Managing editor: Julia Wallace
Production manager: Linnea Knollmueller • Copy editor: Kayla Fenstermaker • Proofreaders:
Cara Iverson and Rachel Kirsch • Art director: Ashley Tucker

Interior book design by Ashley Tucker

For details on special quantity discounts for bulk purchases,
contact specialmarketscms@penguinrandomhouse.com.

PHOTOGRAPHY CREDITS

Valerie Ellis is a children's book author, a speaker, and the founder of the multi-author online resource *Our Everyday Parables,* which offers book reviews and resources for families pursuing faith and compassion.

A certified teacher, Valerie is passionate about helping kids and parents connect with God and one another in the everyday moments. Her books are designed to serve families at the intersection of faith and fun.

Valerie is a member of The MomCo (MOPS International), the Society of Children's Book Writers and Illustrators (SCBWI), and the Texas Library Association. She enjoys hiking, live music, and adventuring with her husband, Josh, and their two boys. Find out more at valerieellis.com.

Jen Bricking is a children's book illustrator and concept artist. She has worked on video games for Disney and Microsoft, and has illustrated numerous middle grade books and picture books. When she's not busy illustrating, she enjoys traveling, skateboarding, and hiking. You can follow her on Instagram @jenbricking and find more art on her website at jenbricking.com.